Praise for

"At the intersection of storytelling and recovery, you meet Anna David."
FORBES MAGAZINE

"Anna David's journey is ripe with wry observation of situations ranging from poignant to hilarious, ending with the ultimate message that we all make our own happy endings."
JEN LANCASTER, *NEW YORK TIMES* BESTSELLING AUTHOR OF *BITTER IS THE NEW BLACK*

"Hysterical and touching…"
PUBLISHER'S WEEKLY

"Anna David writes with a strain of relentless, self-deprecating genius that re-casts the worn-down hooves of Prada-wearing demons with spanking new kicks."
JERRY STAHL, BESTSELLING AUTHOR OF *PERMANENT MIDNIGHT* AND *I, FATTY*

"Funny, smart, and compulsively likeable, Anna David is this decade's answer to Carrie Bradshaw."
ALLISON WINN SCOTCH, *NEW YORK TIMES* BESTSELLING AUTHOR OF *THE DEPARTMENT OF LOST AND FOUND*

"Glitzy, glamorous, gossipy…"
BOOKLIST

"Anna David knows about the power of sharing your story… hilarious, honest, and real."
RYAN HAMPTON, AUTHOR OF *AMERICAN FIX*, NPR COMMENTATOR

"Anna addresses addiction, recovery and modern love in such a funny, honest, caustic and no-holds-barred way, you feel like you've lived it,"
CINDY CHUPACK, EMMY-AWARD WINNING WRITER/EXECUTIVE PRODUCER OF *SEX AND THE CITY*

How to Get Successful By F*cking Up Your Life

Essays on Addiction & Recovery

Anna David

Copyright © 2019 All rights reserved. No part of this publication can be reproduced or transmitted in any form or by any means, electronic or mechanical, without permission in writing from the author or publisher.

ISBN-13: 978-1-7325008-5-3

This work is non-fiction and, as such, reflects the author's memory of the experiences. Many of the names and identifying characteristics of the individuals featured in this book have been changed to protect their privacy and certain individuals are composites. Dialogue and events have been recreated; in some cases, conversations were edited to convey their substance rather than written exactly as they occurred.

For all the other f*ck ups out there: God bless us.

Table of Contents

Introduction 1

Part 1: WHAT IT WAS LIKE

I Ate Space Cakes and Lost My Mind 7
My Three Dealers 13
What Addiction Sounded Like 19
When You're So High That You Think Your Neighbor
is Trying to Kill You 25
My New Millennium New Year 31
That Time I Convinced Myself I Wasn't an Alcoholic 37
Trying to Get Sober Before I Was Trying to Get Sober 43

Part 2: WHAT HAPPENED

My Four-Legged Interventionist 51
I Wasn't a Pill Head But Boy, I Liked Pills 57
Dating as a Newcomer 63
Making Amends Was Everything I Least Expected 69
Nobody Believes Me When I Tell Them I Used to Smoke
Two Packs a Day 77
Babysitting (with) a Movie Star 83
Even Sober, I Was a Nightmare Employee 91
The Yellow Brick Road 103

Part 3: WHAT IT'S LIKE NOW

I'm Addicted to the Internet – So What? 113

Yes, I Believe in God... Except When I Don't 119

Becoming the Person I Drank to Be 123

I'm the Weirdest Codependent in the World 129

What Happens to an Irritable Person on a Meditation Retreat? 135

My Addiction Was a Family Disease 141

Congrats on Quitting Sugar, Now Let Me Act out On My
Addiction in Peace 147

Facing Fear Sober 153

But I Thought the Rules Didn't Apply to Me? 159

Confessions of a So-So Sponsor 165

Party Girl 173

Introduction

I didn't expect to become a down-and-out cocaine addict.

I was raised to be successful.

The problem is, the values I was given for success didn't work for me.

Let's start with this one. My dad always said we lived by the Golden Rule: the one who made the gold made the rules.

I didn't actually know that this was *not* the Golden Rule until I was in my mid-20s. Even if I had, doing unto others as you would have them do unto you wouldn't have been words I'd have understood. Our family philosophy was pretty much "sue them before they can sue you."

I was told that in order to be considered a successful person, you had to get a good enough SAT score to get into Harvard. My dad had scored an 800 on his math SAT, a fact that was treated like lore the same way another family might discuss a grandfather serving in the war.

I was told to make six figures at my first job. My dad had a thriving business by the time he was in his early 20s, another fact that was discussed repeatedly and with great reverence.

This Harvard thing, however, was the most crucial element when it came to belonging in this family, since it was in my DNA: My dad had gone to Harvard. My grandmother went to Radcliffe. My brother, who's two-and-a-half years older than me, went to Harvard.

I did not go to Harvard.

During the application process, I seemed to be the only one in my family who was clear about the fact that I wouldn't get in. My

SAT scores were exceedingly average despite the fact that my dad hired people who wrote SAT books to tutor me. My grades were, by many people's standards, solid. By my family and Harvard's standards, however, they were not.

I ended up at Trinity College, a university which is, by most everybody's standards, a good school—a "Little Ivy." I know this because whenever someone asks me where I went to college and I answer that I didn't go to a good school and then, when pressed, give them the name, they're always seemingly shocked that I'm not proud of it.

I don't expect anyone to weep for me because I couldn't get into the best overpriced college and so I had to go to a not as good overpriced college but my point is that it never occurred to me that I wasn't a complete and utter failure. I didn't understand that success had anything to do with things beyond SAT scores and education and the amount of money you made.

I didn't understand that being loving, being generous and being happy had anything to do with success.

I didn't understand that I could find my own kind of success later in life.

I figured some people were born to be successful and others were not and I was part of the latter group.

Because it was clear to me that I was never going to be able to swim in my family's waters, I focused on the one area where I was highly skilled: having fun.

In particular, having fun with alcohol and drugs.

We all know how these stories go. My particular version had me going from casual use to spending a lot of my 20s holed up by myself doing cocaine, knowing I was killing myself but believing with every cell in my body that sobriety would be worse than death.

I did, however, have one logical thought that saved me: I could always try sobriety and if it was in fact worse than death, I could go ahead and kill myself. But I couldn't kill myself and *then* find that out.

So I tried sobriety and realized it wasn't the end of my life but the beginning.

In the 18 years that have followed, I've had to learn how to navigate a life that involves not being able to escape from my feelings. And I've had to embrace a life that involves continuous growth whether I've felt like growing or not (and usually not).

The truth is I don't work on myself because I'm brave or special. I do it because a life without substances, when you're someone who's addicted to escaping difficult feelings, involves facing extremely uncomfortable emotions at times. And I hate uncomfortable emotions so much that I'll do every form of self-improvement I can find in order to make them go away.

With all that self-improvement has come, to my utter shock, the sort of success I never could have imagined as the B student in the A+ family.

I haven't followed the typical paths. I've been fired from most every job I've ever had. I've sabotaged amazing opportunities.

But at this point in my life I can honestly say I feel successful on all levels…not just with what I've achieved but with how I *feel* about what I've achieved, not to mention how I feel about what I *haven't* achieved.

I mostly feel like a success because I've learned to quiet the negative voice that was nurtured to exponential degrees during my formative years.

And, as the saying goes, if I can do that, anyone can.

The essays gathered here document a lot of my journey…the one from girl who tried to snort away those feelings that she could never measure up to woman who shares about her experiences so she can shed light on them.

The book is divided into three sections that will be familiar to anyone who's ever sat on a folding chair in a church basement drinking bad coffee: What It Was Like (pre-sobriety), What Happened (early sobriety) and What It's Like Now (today). Many of the stories gathered here are ones I told at my monthly storytelling show in Los Angeles. Plenty of them are pieces I published on websites like Psychology Today and The Huffington Post.

The tone is often light and that's for a very specific reason—my entire work and life philosophy is based on the concept that you catch more flies with honey than with vinegar. In other words, I always try to entertain people first and then, when they're laughing, share the sort of truth that has helped save me.

I hope you'll be able to use some of the mistakes I've made as inspiration to feel better about your own (not to mention potential material for your Not To Do list). And I hope you'll see that it's never, ever too late to turn it all around.

Part 1
WHAT IT WAS LIKE

I Ate Space Cakes and Lost My Mind

I am someone who should never have smoked pot.

While other people got silly and fun, I became brooding and introspective. Sure, I could shovel down Cool Ranch Doritos with all the people laughing at the specks they saw on the kitchen counter but the whole time I'd be wondering if they were secretly laughing at me. See, I have a brain that is constantly scanning for negative possibilities, and when it finds one, blows it up billboard size and blasts it into my synapses. With pot, I found a drug that would not only enhance and exacerbate that process but also make me fat.

The expressions "going to the hardware store for milk" or "going back to the empty well for water" are popular among codependents. They're about that thing people do when they know someone—usually a parent—isn't going to give them what they need, but their desire to get their needs met supersedes this knowledge. That was me with pot. Rather than accepting the fact that my brain chemistry caused pot to do the opposite of what it was supposed to, I would go back to the bong-well for more, thinking this time would be different.

And it would be different. Oftentimes it would be worse.

Someone like me should not have gone to Amsterdam for a weekend. But, when I was studying abroad my junior year in college, that's exactly what my flatmate Annie and I did. And, well, on our first day we went to a café and smoked hash and that all seemed to go okay.

But the next day, we wanted to do something different. We wanted to eat space cakes.

We found a café where we got our space cakes, which I remember looking and tasting quite a bit like pound cake—a treat I've always loved. We ate them. I think we may have played Connect Four. I felt totally normal.

"These aren't doing anything," I complained to Annie.

She agreed. And so we did the next logical thing: we ate more. And more. And more. Like I said, pound cake has always been a favorite treat for me and since they weren't doing anything, what did it matter?

An hour or so later, Annie and I decided to go see the movie *Pacific Heights*, a kind of shitty thriller that was playing down the street with English subtitles. Here's what I remember:

We bought tickets. We started watching the movie. It was sort of bad.

Then. There was an intermission.

Does this make sense? No. But it happened.

We filed out with everyone else into the lobby. And that's when everything went well not quite sideways and not quite upside down but like a Rubik's Cube that was being violently twisted by a demonic nine-year old. I held the wall as everything around me began to take on a funhouse mirror look.

"Dude," Annie said.

"I know."

There were no other words. I didn't know how to form the sentence "I'm as high as I've ever been."

So we went back in the theater and watched the rest of the movie.

Afterwards we walked out, clinging to each other the way an elderly couple might. Neither of us said a word. Then, Annie said she had to pee.

I remembered just then that I had forgotten about bodily functions and, now that I remembered, I really needed to pee, too.

We went into a Burger King bathroom and standing there handing out towels, like it was the Four Seasons, was a bathroom attendant.

This seemed like the funniest and craziest thing imaginable, so much so that I started laughing so hard that I began to fall over. And so I did the next logical thing: I allowed myself to fall so I could bang my hand on the ground, like I was having a tantrum. It occurred to me that I could be dying. As I remember it, the bathroom attendant—if there was a bathroom attendant, this whole thing could have been in my head—said something about calling security.

Annie pulled me off the floor, I managed to pee and we started walking back to the hotel. Then we heard Madonna's "Vogue" playing out of a club we passed. Without saying a word to each other, we ran inside. It was winter and we were college students with tons of stuff on us so, once we were in the middle of the dance floor, we tossed off our backpacks, our coats, our purses, our scarves, our hats and our mittens and, per Madonna's instructions, struck a pose. Then the song ended. We looked around the club. It felt like 100 Dutch folks were staring at the crazy Americans who'd run in there, tossed off their worldly possessions like they were on fire and tried to dance to a song that was over. As we silently picked our things up, I realized that the reason they were looking at us so warily is that this was not in fact a club but a restaurant that happened to be playing Madonna and we'd just run into the middle of it, tossed everything we had on the floor and posed.

We decided the only safe thing for us to do was go back to our hostel, where we set the alarm for 7 am the next morning so we could make our 9 am flight.

I fell asleep in an instant and the next thing I knew, it was morning. I opened my eyes, feeling like a fat man was sitting on me. But when I looked at the clock, I was thrilled: it was 6:30 am. We'd beaten the alarm!

Feeling proud, I got up and stumbled to the door to retrieve the newspaper the hotel had left. I looked at it. There was something about it that was strange.

"This is so weird," I said to Annie, who had just opened her eyes. "Today's paper has tomorrow's date."

"What?"

We looked at each other. We looked at the paper. And we both knew: The paper did not decide to randomly print the next day's date. We had not only slept through the alarm but nearly 40 hours—through the night, through the next day and then through the following night. Space cakes had not only possibly caused permanent brain damage but had also made me lose a day of my life.

I wish I could say I left pot alone after that. But I didn't. That empty well was going to deliver me water someday, God damn it. That hardware store would have a milk special, I just knew it. So let's just say that the fact that my sobriety doesn't allow me to smoke pot isn't much of a sacrifice.

I still enjoy pound cake and Connect Four and Vogue-ing. Some things, thank God, I didn't have to give up.

My Three Dealers

I remember the day I figured out all I needed to be happy.

I was sitting on my couch in the middle of a Saturday when I suddenly realized why my emotions were always so all over the place.

It was that I was entirely too dependent on other people.

To do cocaine.

Back then, I never had coke of my own and so I spent parties going up to fellow drug users asking if they were holding. If they were, hallelujah! I could do coke with them and be happy. If they weren't, then I couldn't.

I needed to be more in control of my emotions.

I needed, I realized, my own cocaine dealer.

While today there's surely a cocaine dealer app, even back in the late 90s, getting one of these wasn't as difficult as you might think. Or it might have been if you were a mother of two in Ames, Iowa, but if you were a 20-something Angelino who had done coke with any number of people over the previous few years, you made a few calls and were gifted with your very own dopamine increaser: in my case, Jose, a Mexican man who would show up, usually within the hour, with grams folded into Lotto tickets—his signature wrapping and a gesture I appreciated. Jose's only drawback, aside from the fact that his coke tasted so much like gasoline that all you could do when you snorted it was imagine the gas tanks it was transported in, was that he made you buy two grams at a time. Dude wasn't doing deliveries for a mere $60. $120 and then you were talking.

And so I made due with Jose, even though his coke was so bad that the best part was the half hour between texting him and his arrival, when I could be in gleeful anticipation.

Then I caught a lucky break. One night I was out with a few friends and we ended up at a strip club.

I walked into this place, drunk, and upon seeing women stripping from a stage, thought I should maybe be stripping too. Drunk logic is awesome, isn't it? And so—this part is a little fuzzy but I think I removed my top and attempted to climb onto the stage. The manager—a severe brunette who introduced herself as Vera—approached me and asked me to come with her. I assumed I was in trouble.

But I was not in trouble; turns out Vera wanted to bond. She gestured to the bathroom and once we were in there, she pulled out a stash of coke, which she invited me to do with her. I marveled at the fact that she knew I'd be open to this but if you're the manager of a strip club and a drunk girl walks in, takes her top off and tries to walk onto the stage, you can probably conclude that girl likes to party.

It was pretty much the best coke I'd ever done. Or let's not be dramatic: it wasn't as horrific as the Jose petroleum experience.

My conversation with Vera went like this:

"Wow, this coke is great!"

"Isn't it?"

"Yes!"

"I have more."

"You do?"

"Oh, yes. A lot more. I sell it for $70 a gram."

"Wow. That's great. I wish I had cash on me."

"There's an ATM right outside this bathroom."

And that's how I found my second dealer.

Vera, to be clear, wasn't an ideal dealer. Yes, she wrapped her cocaine in bright pink Post-Its, which was far more feminine than Jose's Lotto tickets. But she lived across town and didn't deliver. Plus, there was a level of girl talk that always seemed to be required during transactions with her, something that was never a part of my interactions with Jose, who only spoke Spanish.

Vera's girl talk wasn't really about men or dating or shopping or whatever else you might consider girl talk. No, Vera was a businesswoman and she wanted to share her million dollar ideas. I remember my writing partner and I sitting on her couch one day listening to her tell us she was going to get rich off a round towel she'd invented—something that every sun bather in the world would eat up, she explained, because they wouldn't have to adjust their towel as the sun moved across the sky.

Vera wanted us to invest in her company. Vera was getting to be too much.

Luckily, shortly after that, I was out one night with a friend who had a number listed in her phone under "Trouble," because that's what she would get in if she was actually using it. Trouble was Sal, an Italian dealer whose signature move didn't involve Lotto tickets or pink Post-Its but did involve the fact that you could do coke with him during your purchase, as a sort of wine tasting, see-what-you're-getting perk. Of course, you weren't tasting the coke, you were just taking advantage of a freebie because you always knew what you were getting with Sal, and it sucked. You didn't go to Sal because you were looking for the highest quality. You went to him because you didn't want the two grams Jose required and you needed a break from Vera. Or because you were more broke than usual. His grams went for $40.

By the time I was calling Sal, the drugs had more than stopped working. There were few things sadder than sitting in Sal's living room passing around a plate with lines of the worst coke imaginable. But even then, my denial was strong enough for me to think there wasn't anything wrong with what I was doing. I remember one day a girl walked in and when she left the room, another girl whispered that Sal shouldn't sell to her because, after all, *she'd been in rehab.*

"Rehab?!" I remember asking in shock. "Rehab?" This girl, I realized, clearly had a problem!

The other girl nodded and we looked at each other in solidarity: we, after all, were simply two girls doing coke in the middle of the day at a strange man's apartment. That other girl, we decided with a mutually understood form of denial neither of us were conscious of at the time, had a problem.

It wasn't long after that the depression and horror of how I was living caught up with me and I was the one who ended up in rehab. And when I walked in on my first day, guess who was sitting there in the office, also checking in?

Vera. Yep.

When she saw me, she gestured for me to follow her outside. "Look, they can't know I dealt to you, got it?" she said. "Just say we know each other from temple, okay?"

"What?"

"I'm here because I got busted. I'm fighting it. I was never your dealer. Got it?"

I got it. And then we were in treatment together. She was kind of a fun rehab mate, always into smoke breaks and gossiping, but we lost touch after we were discharged and I have no idea what happened to her, not to mention Jose or Sal.

Still, when I think of Vera, I know how I like to picture her: sitting on a tropical island somewhere, lounging on a large round towel.

What Addiction Sounded Like

I was not someone who should have liked cocaine. I've always been very energetic, very jittery, very wired. If I was going to do a drug with enthusiasm, it should have been pot or acid or mushrooms or even Ecstasy. But pot just made me paranoid that no one understood what it was I was trying to say—a fear exacerbated by the fact that when I was high, I made almost no sense so no one *did* understand what I was trying to say. Mushrooms and Ecstasy were okay but didn't give me that kick. And I had as much interest in acid as I did in bathing in hot wax: expanding my mind so that I could go deeper into myself, have profound realizations and maybe imagine some spiders? Ugh. I was born far deeper into myself than I ever wanted to be. I wanted the opposite. I wanted out.

Cocaine got me out. It made me the me I'd always wanted to be: me, but euphoric. Everything, from whatever cigarette I happened to be smoking to whatever fact I happened to be expounding on (and, in the initial years, I expounded on a lot of facts), excited me. Cocaine made me fall in love with myself—a state unimagined during all those years of subconscious yet crippling self-recrimination. While falling in love with myself surely made me annoying company, this wasn't a problem in the beginning since I was surrounded by many others who were having similar self love affairs and we were all happy to co-exist together. It can be depressing when everyone around you is in love—unless you, too, are in the same boat. In those early days, the group of us could remain confident that we all had someone to love and were also loved back.

The center, of course, could not hold.

People who are utterly convinced of their own brilliance can become tiresome, particularly if they're competing with your cocaine-addled brain for airtime. No, you find yourself wanting to say, the idea of starting a website where we give people financial advice based on their astrological signs is not a good one. No, you realize, you don't think the group of you should consider starting a band, seeing as none of you play instruments or sing. These people, you suddenly realize, are losers.

You don't think of yourself as a loser at this point. At least, you're doing your best not to think of yourself this way. The solution, as you see it, is to stop hanging out with these people.

The solution is to do coke alone.

The first time I stayed up by myself all night, high, I wrote a brilliant television spec script.

It was for *Third Rock From The Sun*, a show I'd never seen, but no matter. I was writing the Hollywood way—by studying other people's scripts in the hopes of mimicking one enough while also injecting enough of myself into it for my words to rise from the bottom of the slush pile to the top.

I started by pouring cocaine onto the framed print my mom had given me, slicing it into lines and inhaling a few in the name of getting my creative juices flowing. That's when I suddenly came up with a genius idea for an episode of *Third Rock*. Which led to me writing the genius episode that night.

Initially, it was surprising when the birds started chirping and I heard my neighbor leave for work. People who are addicted to coke, I would come to learn, are greeted each morning by birds creating a cacophony of cheer so far from their own state of mind at that time of the morning that somehow they make suicide sound like a reasonable escape. But this realization came later. That morning, after completing my brilliant spec script, the birds sounded lovely—like a harbinger of joyous news to come. Television writing jobs. Riches. New friends. Happiness. If I needed cocaine to help make that happen, I remember reasoning, so be it.

Alas, it was not to be. My *Third Rock* spec script was not decreed the paean of brilliance I'd been sure it would be. (I still maintain that it's a damn fine effort.) But, even worse, my writing system—do two lines to get the creative juices flowing followed by two more lines every 20 minutes or so for the following eight to 14 hours in order to keep the flow happening—became instantly ineffective.

The next time I sat down to write, I couldn't do it. And by "it," I mean move. Cocaine, the drug that had once made me ebullient, transforming every lampshade into a potential hat and keeping the party going all night long, betrayed me even further. It made me unable to do anything but sit in front of my computer and shake.

I'd be crouched there, thinking about how badly I had to pee, really wanting to get up and go to the bathroom. But I'd be too jittery to stand up. Or too frightened. So I'd just stay there and shake. I was capable of some movements: I could wipe my nose and chain smoke and even occasionally rise to peer out the window at the neighbors—a composer and his wife, do-gooders who I was convinced spied on me with binoculars.

One movement I could not make, alas, involved tapping keys on the keyboard. I'd stare at the screen, at the Great American Screenplay I'd convinced myself I was writing. And I'd have a lot of ideas for how to make it better. Too many of them, alas. I'd want to try one but there was the shaking to contend with and just the fact that I couldn't seem to find a way to tap the letters out. Still, I'll say one thing for me: I never gave up. I never said, "Gosh, this writing while wired thing isn't working out. Maybe I should watch a movie." I just stayed there and kept trying.

The worst part of it all, as I saw it, was that the way my computer worked was if you didn't hit a key for 60 seconds, a box would pop onto the screen asking if you wanted to save. The question would be accompanied by a beep. Now I don't know how loud a beep it was—how loud I would consider it today—but I know this: in the state I was in, that noise sounded like a megaphone inside a microphone inside my ear. And so I lived in fear of the beep. It somehow symbolized just how bad things were. If I could avoid the beep, I somehow thought, that meant everything was okay.

I couldn't avoid the beep.

I'd sit there, huddled, telling myself to just hit a key—any key!—so I could buy myself some time. But there was a disconnect between my brain and my hand and it wouldn't happen. I'd be in fearful anticipation, thinking, "Do something or the beep will come…the beep is coming...Dear God, it's getting closer...Do something now!" But nothing would happen and then— BEEP!

I'd nearly jump out of my skin, every time. And then I'd spend the next 59 seconds or so trying to avoid the next beep, and miss it.

I'm not sure how long it took me to realize I was depressed. I'd been down for so long that I forgot what not feeling down felt like. The fact that I had a propensity for depression, that depression was in my family, was in my blood, and that depressants like alcohol and cocaine were surely exacerbating that, wasn't something I could afford to think about. I needed cocaine—and though I told myself I didn't need alcohol, I had no interest in giving it up, either. I needed cocaine even though it had gotten to the point where I'd buy it, flush it in a fit of shame, and then call my dealer for more. I needed it when it left me living in fear of a beep I couldn't escape.

It began to dawn on me that my relationship with cocaine was less than healthy. I had, I could admit, an issue with it. I don't think I was comfortable using the word "addiction." But I knew that if I had the drug on me, I couldn't stop ingesting it until the supply was drained and I had the additional problem of not being able to resist calling my dealer to replenish. I knew what had to be done.

I understood that drugs and alcohol were doing this to me but I was certain I couldn't live without them.

I quit cocaine. It wasn't easy, but I did it.

Of course, I needed some comfort through this deprivation, so I allowed myself to drink. And, in fact, I drank quite a bit because my alcohol consumption had increased with all the cocaine use— only because I needed it to come down—and what with giving up coke and everything, I didn't see why I should make myself suffer needlessly by trying to tone down the drinking.

A month passed. And I reasoned that no one who has an issue with cocaine gives up the drug for an entire 30 days.

And so I went back to using it.

I did the quitting-for-a-month thing a few more times. The experiments had variations: during one, a guy I was dating, a pill popper, told me he thought I had a problem, so I asked another guy to take me to a 12-step meeting. God, I hated it. The people I met there all insisted that there was no way I could have an issue with cocaine but not with alcohol, even when I tried explaining how little I enjoyed drinking anymore. But, I reasoned, I could go along with their program. I could be sober.

I made it 10 days.

Ten days where I was regularly taking the Vicodin that my then-boyfriend agreed to share. After 10 days, I'd had enough. Fuck sobriety, I said, really believing I'd been sober.

That was over 18 years ago. The 12-step program I hated so much at first glance has come to save my life. This doesn't mean that I now see sunshine and rainbows where I once only saw darkness and jittery nights. I still experience depression—just not nearly as often as I used to and I almost always understand that it's going to pass. Essentially, I have a real life—one filled with pain and hope and panic and peace and, at times, the instant pain relief and euphoria that alcohol and then cocaine once gave me. I'm still a writer, but now I actually do it. My fingers don't hover over the keyboard, unable to move.

I haven't heard The Beep in over 18 years. Luckily, I still remember exactly how it sounds.

When You're So High That You Think Your Neighbor is Trying to Kill You

When I lived in West Hollywood in my late 20s, my behavior was pretty much standard for the time and era—if you were a gay man in his late teens and early 20s. See I couldn't really find any straight people my age who liked to party the right way and so my group was pretty much gay men, all a good decade younger than me.

We were an interesting crowd. And by interesting I mean not interesting at all. All we had in common was a desire to sit around my then friend Kevin's apartment, passing a plate of cocaine back and forth and taking turns talking and not listening to each other. Conveniently, as if the devil himself had arranged the geography, Kevin only lived two blocks away from me.

Kevin's best friend was a woman named Yani. Now when I say woman, allow me to explain that I had never met a transsexual person before and I didn't realize that state of affairs had actually changed—until about six months into hanging with this new crowd when Yani and I went into the bathroom at a party to do coke.

All was normal until she said she had to pee and suddenly I saw penis. I was more confused than shocked. Had the topic of Yani having a penis not come up during our previous months of doing coke and talking all night at Kevin's apartment? While people on cocaine are not heralded for their listening skills, I imagined I would have been able to stop my yammering long enough to take *that* fact in.

A few weeks later, I decided to throw myself a birthday party at a bar. I told people not to bring presents unless those presents were drugs but drug addicts aren't known for their generosity—or for taking direction. The lone exceptions were Kevin and Yani. Kevin whispered in my ear right when he got there, "Come to the bathroom with me." He opened up his hand to show me a baggie filled with white powder and added, "I stole this coke from my roommate."

As any true lady can attest, it's better when your gifts *aren't* stolen but who was I to be judge-y? Kevin laid out the white lines on top of the toilet and into my nose those lines went.

Very quickly, I realized that things were not as they were supposed to be. For one, I couldn't talk. For another, I couldn't stand. Because of these two factors, I decided to lie down and because the party was crowded, the only place I could find to do that in peace was next to the dumpster behind the bar. Talking and standing continued to feel challenging and so I spent the celebration of my 28th birthday lying by this dumpster with friends occasionally popping out of the party to come wish me a happy birthday. No one seemed remotely surprised to find me celebrating my birthday supine and lying next to the trash.

But it wasn't always wild nights out, randomly discovering a gal pal had a penis, or going into a K-hole by a dumpster for my birthday. (Oh yeah…when Kevin's roommate ended up going to rehab for Special K, we realized *that* had been the drug that had made me comatose. So: horse tranquilizers = not for me. Live and learn!)

The problem is I wasn't learning anything and I was barely living. And the person this perhaps impacted the most was my neighbor Henry.

Henry didn't *just* live next door to me. We actually shared a front door and our apartments were only separated by a staircase. Now you might think, as Henry surely did when he moved in, that a staircase was *plenty* of separation for two dwellings. And it would have been, had I not been the worst neighbor in the history of West Hollywood (which is no small award to grant myself).

My two biggest offenses were giving copies of our front door keys to about 20 coke addicts I knew so they could come and go as they pleased, at all hours. My other offense? I was entertaining those same sort of people at all hours. And by entertaining I mean inviting them over to do coke.

The vitriol Henry felt for me was easy to recognize, seeing as he yelled "SHUT UP!" during my impromptu parties and slammed doors when the yelling didn't do anything. But somehow, despite being the one causing the *entire* problem, I justified my "side" of the story.

The story I told myself was that Henry was mean and violent. Who else but a violent person would slam so many doors? And one night, when I was home doing what any nice girl would—cocaine all alone—I turned on A&E and saw something that chilled me. It was a special called "Neighbors Who Kill" and it featured story after story about seemingly normal people who had been brought to fits of homicidal rage by those living next door to them. The longer I watched this special, the more convinced I became that Henry was on the verge of murdering me. This show was like televised WebMD, if your paranoia was focused less on whether or not your mole was cancerous and more on if your neighbor was sharpening his ax for you.

The fact that I was doing a gram of cocaine by myself did not, to be clear, help eradicate my paranoia. By the time I was finished, I was convinced it was my last night on earth. I called a bunch of friends to tell them, and they all said versions of "I promise you don't have anything to worry about" and "Just go to sleep." Finally, I got a hold of the two people who would understand: Kevin and Yani.

"Oh my God!" Kevin shrieked when I told him about the special and how I was reasonably certain Henry was going to kill me. "You are not safe there! We're going to walk over and save you."

And they did! Like the insane person I was, I was worried that Henry would kill my two cats if I was not there so I put each of them in cat carriers and walked with Kevin and Yani back to his place, where we did coke until sunrise and talked about how lucky I was to have had my life saved. We also concluded that I needed a plan if I was going to be able to stay alive.

And so we decided that I should *call the cops*. Yes, once I returned from Kevin's place with my cats, still high, I called 911 and reported that I had a dangerous neighbor. And so that's how I found myself, mid coke-drip, explaining the situation—the door slamming, the A&E special, my conviction that my life was in danger—to two not terribly sympathetic officers.

I didn't tell them about my part in the situation but I could nevertheless tell that these cops weren't remotely concerned for my life. They wrote down a number for a local neighbor dispute center and told me to have a good day.

I did not have a good day or many good days ever during that particular period of time. But years later, after I'd gotten sober, made amends to Henry and we'd become friends, we walked down that shared staircase on a Sunday morning to go shopping together.

Turns out we were in for a surprise. See, I had gotten a new couch a few weeks before and had moved my old one to the space in our garage in front of where I parked. And that particular morning, there was a *naked man* sitting on it. And not just sitting on it but sitting on it and deeply, deeply annoyed at us for disturbing him. He was clearly on serious drugs, thinking that he was if not home then at least somewhere that he was supposed to be naked, and we were two rude gawkers making him very angry. Within a few seconds, he stood up and ran away.

I couldn't help but laugh. I knew the look on this man's face so well...the justification, the conviction he was in the right despite every bit of logic in the world indicating that this was not so—all of it.

Henry didn't seem so amused. Do you blame him?

My New Millennium New Year

The December before I got sober, my mom and stepdad traded their house for an apartment in Paris so they could spend the holiday in the City of Lights. It was a lovely idea and would have stayed a lovely idea had they not invited me. It was 1999, Prince's favorite year, and so the plan was to go in early December and stay for the Millennium New Year's Eve. Some people said the world was going to end. Others said computers were all going to go haywire. I wasn't really listening to much people were saying at that point because I spent most of the time with my head over a mirror using a rolled-up dollar bill to snort whatever was on that mirror, and then talking at whoever was around about my amazing business and life ideas. I was so out of it in terms of what was going on in the world that one time around then when I did go to a party and someone mentioned Viagra, I asked what that was and the entire room stopped.

"Are you serious?" someone asked. I was. That's how I learned that something was a big deal. When no one could believe I didn't know what it was. That's about when I decided to spend most of my time alone.

Point is, I didn't know much about what people were saying would happen when the clock struck Jan 1, 2000. I just knew that Paris sounded glamorous. My only issue was: how was I going to bring coke on the plane?

That was answered quickly. I wasn't. I'd seen *Midnight Express*. I was going to have to figure something out when I got there.

As luck would have it, I arrived the night before my parents and a lovely American girl named Alice let me into the apartment. I can't say for sure that she was lovely because my opinion was highly influenced by the fact that once I'd put my bags down, she asked me my favorite question at the time: Want to go out for a drink?

Because I could sniff out fellow drug users the way a dog can sense an earthquake, within roughly 20 minutes of descending on a club with Alice, I'd found my target: Alexandre, a French photographer who could be considered cute if you had a certain number of drinks in you. As I talked to him, I got that number of drinks in me and started to also find him vaguely charming. Even when he told me that by "photographer," he meant "nude photographer," I decided that was sexy and appealing. But really what I found most alluring about him was his answer when I asked him where I could buy some coke. "It's very expensive here," he told me in his strong French accent. "But you don't need to buy it. All my friends do it so just spend time with me."

Now I'm a girl who likes to save her francs and this plan also meant not having to worry about the risk of getting busted by my mom and step dad (my mom, having learned by being, well, my mother, had some experience with rifling through my drawers and discovering illegal substances).

And thus began my month of infiltrating the seedy underbelly of Parisian artists. Every night, Alexandre would pick me up and take me over to his friend Serge's apartment, which was always filled with both drug addicts and drugs. None of them spoke English and while I'd started studying French at the age of five, by the time I got to French Lit class my senior year in high school, I was smoking pot before every class and pretending ink was coming from my fingers and not from my pens, never speaking up in class, buying every book in English and writing all my papers using a French-English dictionary. In the process, I'd managed to unlearn everything I'd been taught over the previous decade.

Luckily, I could understand what they were saying to me if they spoke slowly and I stopped them a few times. Plus when I had alcohol and drugs in me, I felt like I could speak fluently. And to my credit, these people did seem to understand me well enough, though I wasn't saying anything too interesting or complex. There was a lot of "Je pense que, God damn it, how do you say 'I want a drink'? Bu? Ahhh…Cigarette? Never mind!" And then I'd plop back on a couch and someone would pass me a mirror and a dollar bill.

We'd stay up all night long and every morning, somewhere between 6 and 8 am, Alexandre and I would leave Serge's and he'd drop me off at my parents' temporary apartment. I'd walk past my family while they were in the kitchen prepping to go to the Eiffel Tower. Then I'd take a bunch of Ambien, sleep all day and go out with Alexandre again that night.

Ugh, my poor mother. At first she tried to put a positive spin on my behavior. "Isn't it amazing the way Anna can go anywhere and make friends?" Mom would say over dinner, usually just a few hours after I woke up. "We're only here a few days and she's already getting phone calls from locals!" Then her attitude changed. She cornered me in the hallway one evening and asked, "How many of these are you taking?" as she held up a bottle of Ambien she'd found. I mumbled something about how she needed to stop judging me and then told her I was late. It was Serge's 30th birthday and he was celebrating by having 30 people over to drink 30 bottles of Dom Perignon.

That night, Serge came up to me while I was dancing by myself to Jewel's "Hands" in the kitchen (horrifying, the things you can't forget no matter how hard you try) and asked me what I was planning to do for New Year's Eve. Since these guys were my entire social life there, I said, "I don't know, what are we doing?" But I said it in Franclais so it was something like, "Je ne sais pas. Quelle est la plan?" He lowered his voice and told me that his wife, who was a flight attendant and had been traveling the whole month, was coming back on the 31st. She happened to also be named Anna, he explained. Then he rushed right to the offer: he'd shown her my photo and they wanted to know if I'd be interested in a New Year's Eve ménage. I was not, he added, to tell Alexandre.

I weighed it. I'd never been with a woman but I'd never spent a month hanging out with the seedy underbelly of Paris either. It would make a good story: go into the millennium going down on a woman for the first time. I can't claim I found it that sexually exciting. Though I think the concept of two women together is erotic, I really am one of the straightest women I know. Or maybe I'm just a little too old for bisexuality; "gay in college" became a thing only after I graduated from college.

I still had a few days to decide if I was going to join Serge and Anna and trust me when I tell you that I spent those days in pretty much the shadiest ways possible. Don't believe me? What about when I tell you that one of those days was spent snorting heroin with Alexandre and then doing a nude photo shoot? Yep. The most horrifying part about this isn't that I was doing it but the fact that I was about 20 pounds heavier than I am now and look, if you're going to do a nude heroin shoot, you better be god damn emaciated. And because I am a chronic confessionalist, I told my mom and step dad what I was doing, though I wasn't insane so I did edit out the heroin part. Literally, I was like, "Hey mom, I'll see you later, going to take some nude photos at Alexandre's!"

I ended up saying no to Serge and missing out on his generous wife-sharing offer. I also ended up giving the nude photos to my mom in an album (completely disproving the statement I just made about how I wasn't insane). I also ended up in rehab the following May. While all of this does make a good story (cocaine, seedy but glamorous Parisians, nude photos, ménage offers), the truth is this: I was as lost and broken as I've ever been. My truly amazing stepdad died just a few years later and so time I could have spent walking around one of the world's most beautiful cities with him and my mom, I spent dancing by myself, high as could be, to Jewel's "Hands." And I remember the sadness I felt when taking those photos, thinking, "This was not what was supposed to happen to my life. What the fuck happened?"

So, while the world didn't end in 2000, mine sort of did.

I don't have any idea what came of Alexandre and Serge and Anna and the lot of them. Alexandre was a complete Luddite who didn't even have an email address so there was no keeping up. The best part about that—what I think we can all be grateful for—is that Luddites don't have any idea what the Internet even is. And so the only person who got to see those (fat) nude photos is my poor mother, who hopefully burned them.

That Time I Convinced Myself I Wasn't an Alcoholic

They say a relapse happens long before you take the drink.

In my case they were right.

I can actually trace my relapse to a specific moment.

I was six-and-a-half months sober and still going to outpatient meetings at my rehab when my best friend from rehab, a guy who was gay but hadn't come out of the closet yet, and who I had a mad crush on, shared about having relapsed on coke.

I took him aside after the meeting and asked him everything I wanted to know: Had it been fun at first and then terrible? Did he hear the birds chirp and want to kill himself? Had it all been a mistake?

"No," he said. "It was fantastic. I don't think I'm an addict."

Part of me thought I must have misheard him. Wasn't relapse supposed to feel devastating? Wasn't a head full of AA and a body full of booze (or coke) supposed to be the worst feeling in the world?

But I also understood what he was saying. See, I'd been theorizing that I wasn't an alcoholic. I was someone who liked cocaine very much, that was clear. I was also a person who enjoyed her Ambien and pain pills. And sure, of course, I drank. Quite a bit. Anyone doing the amount of coke I was doing would have to in order to not jump out of her skin. I had been reasonably certain from the moment I entered rehab that I was an addict and *not* an alcoholic, but people didn't seem to understand this distinction, no matter how many times I tried to explain it to them.

A few nights later, I was at a silly Hollywood party and ran into a guy I had dated who had been sober when I was a raging coke party girl. I had been stupidly hung up on him, despite the fact that he'd broken up with me by simply disappearing one day and then later telling me that his reason had been that I needed to wax—down there.

But anyway, I saw him and launched into this whole thing about how I was now sober and now I understood his sobriety and he, probably thinking of nothing but my hairy nether regions (PS: I now laser), informed me that he was no longer, in fact, sober.

I was shocked. This guy, the one I'd decided years earlier was the coolest guy in the world (for the record, I still know him today and he's the furthest thing from the coolest guy in the world) was no longer sober? How cool could sobriety be, I wondered, if my best friend from rehab and the coolest guy in the world were so cavalier about not drinking the Kool-Aid anymore and, in fact, drinking instead?

An hour or so later, I ran into a guy I knew—an agent that reeked of agent, which is to say that he had the sort of personality where he couldn't have been anything *but* an agent. He was not a good person. He was not an attractive person. He was, however, a person who, that night, asked me out. Under normal circumstances, I would have ducked out of this. But, I saw later, these were not normal circumstances. These were circumstances where my addict brain was coming up with a plan.

"Sure," I said, passing along my number.

"I could make us dinner," he said. "This Saturday night."

"Sounds great," I responded, knowing full well that "I could make us dinner this Saturday night" was agent speak for "I am planning to have sex with you this Saturday night and you will probably go along with it because I'm a powerful agent."

That Saturday, I got what felt like a sudden desire to drink. A very strong desire. I would have a drink at dinner with this man, I decided. It was that simple a decision. Then I had the thought that since I was going to have a drink with this man that night, maybe I should have a drink right then? It was about noon and I could go get a bottle of wine. I recognized this thought as one that sounded incredibly alcoholic. And since I was not an alcoholic, I ignored it and pretended I never had it. I realized that I was at a crucial juncture and this juncture involved calling my sponsor—that, in fact, one of the main reasons sponsors existed was so that we could call them at moments like this.

I opted not to call her.

But since not calling *anyone* to inform them of my plan sounded like an incredibly alcoholic thing to do, I did make a call.

I called a guy I knew who was sober. A guy I'd dated who was sober. A guy I'd dated who was sober and now had a girlfriend. I told him I wanted to drink. He said all the things you're supposed to say. He told me that I could always do it tomorrow if I still wanted to. He did not say, "Let me leave my girlfriend's and come over and make sure you don't drink" and because of that, I felt I had permission to carry out my plan. I had informed another sober person of my plan and he had not stopped me.

I went to the agent who couldn't have not been an agent's house. Within a few moments of walking in, I touched a bottle of red sitting on his counter. "Remember how I told you I don't drink?" I asked him. (I told everyone, often people who couldn't have cared less, that I didn't drink.) He nodded. I said, "Yeah, well I'm not doing *that* anymore. Can I have a glass?"

His eyes lit up like a Christmas tree. The one obstacle that had sat between him and his plan to have sex with a girl simply because he was an agent—my sobriety—had disintegrated into thin air. "Absolutely!" he said.

And so I had a glass of wine. Nothing about that sip was dramatic. It was the opposite of dramatic. *This* beverage was why I'd been sitting in church basements for the past six months discussing my issues? The agent commented that from the way I was drinking, it was clear I didn't have a drinking problem. I was hardly chugging. I agreed. I helped myself to another glass. And another. Until I'd had a couple bottles.

Later—it could have been an hour, it could have been two—I was sitting on some bench sort of thing in his foyer. He was sitting next to me. That's when he busted out with, "I don't feel bad for giving you alcohol. But I do feel bad about the drugs."

I was confused. Had he drugged me? Then I looked at his hand which was, conveniently enough, right in front of my face. It was filled with pills. Ecstasy pills.

"Oh, I can't do Ex," I responded. "My problem was with drugs. I..." I had planned to launch into something about my dedication to not doing drugs since I was a drug addict and not an alcoholic but I didn't have a chance to do that because my mouth was busy swallowing Ecstasy. Yup. Without even a second thought. And then, well I don't know about you, but Ecstasy never hit fast enough and when something doesn't happen fast enough I tend to think, still today, that it's not going to happen at all. And, well, I'd done drugs so the wheels had clearly already fallen off the bus and so I guess I figured WTF and took another. After another span of time—possibly a few minutes, possibly an hour—I still didn't feel much and so I did the next logical thing and took another.

Here's the thing: I was high but not *that* high. I remember it all. I remember going up and down the floors in his house—I think there were three—and maybe going in a sauna in my clothes and then chattering incessantly to him outside while chain-smoking and him telling me I was so fun to listen to that I should probably have my own TV show, a brilliant agent line if ever there was one, and I know this is crazy and it really is a testament to how truly unappealing this man was but I DID NOT HAVE SEX WITH HIM. One relapse, two bottles of wine and three hits of Ecstasy in a mansion and this man could still not get laid. Not for lack of effort either. I remember sitting again on that bench thing in the foyer and him telling me that it was 4 am and I obviously couldn't drive home so I should definitely stay over but not to worry, I could stay in a guest room, and him telling me this in between trying to caress my face. And then I remember that I, sober as a person under these conditions possibly could be, stood up.

"I'm going home," I told him.

"You can't," he responded.

"But I am," I said. "And," I added, "You really should get a better drug dealer."

And I went home.

No, it wasn't smart driving under those conditions. No, it wasn't smart taking those drugs. But I went back to a meeting the following day, identified myself as a newcomer and started actually doing what had been suggested to me from the beginning. My life got roughly 10,000 times better. It was about a year into sobriety that I realized I'd always drank alcoholically. My vision of the world had just been so small and the people I'd surrounded myself with so similar to me that I'd had no idea.

I've stayed sober since. And while I recognize that as a great accomplishment, I don't want to discount one other: in all that time, I've still managed to never sleep with an agent.

Trying to Get Sober Before I Was Trying to Get Sober

There would come a time when, no matter how vehemently I was convinced that AA was where Jesus freaks went to chain smoke, talk about the good old days and just in general be losers, I would become willing to check it out. All my methods to stop using—keeping coke at other people's houses, going on trips to places where I didn't have dealers, flushing coke only to call my dealer immediately after—would fail and so I would be desperate enough to try.

Now this was the Internet dark ages, comparatively speaking, which is to say that there was no 12-step directory online or information out there about rehab, aside from gossip magazine stories on people like Charlie Sheen, which were essentially advertisements for

Promises and Betty Ford. But one morning, after one seriously long night, I pored through what I could find online and discovered that there was a meeting near me that started in the next half hour.

To be clear, I have never been good with numbers or directions, to the point that I have diagnosed myself with something I call "directional dyslexia." My brain just can't process information having to do with numbers and streets. I zipped over to the address I could swear I read and it was…

John and Pete's Liquor Store, between Melrose and Santa Monica.

"A liquor store," I thought. "Well, that's kitschy."

As I considered it, I realized it certainly made sense that someone who owned a liquor store would drink to excess and need help but not want to give up the day job or sell the business. Maybe John or Pete or whoever thought he could really help others by being here, right in the eye of the tiger or something, I thought. Or maybe AA had a sense of humor so they held their meetings in liquor stores! (This isn't, of course, that far off from the idea that there are meetings in bars and clubs but I didn't know that then.)

As I walked into the liquor store, however, it was clear that no meeting was afoot. Then I noticed that behind the store was an apartment. That must be, I decided, where the meetings were held. I approached the guy behind the counter.

"Um, is the meeting back there?" I asked him.

He looked at me, confused. "The meeting?" he asked.

God damn it, I thought. There was clearly a code word. I knew AA was fucked up.

I was about to say "The AA meeting" but realized I was too ashamed to get the words out of my mouth. And so I just muttered, "Never mind," concluded that AA was not only full of losers but also exclusionary, which was the greatest irony imaginable, and justified hating AA for quite a while afterwards. Even when I looked up the address later and realized I had morphed a street of one meeting with an address number of another, I still justified hating AA.

And then the day came when I was desperate enough to try again. This time, I was going to make sure I wasn't headed to a liquor store for some secret meeting. This time, I decided to try Cocaine Anonymous. I looked up meeting information and saw that there was one on 3rd Street. Now I had, in my early days in LA, logged some serious time on this very adorable section of 3rd street and so I figured I would be attending a cute and potentially stylish meeting filled with others who enjoyed the 3rd street West Hollywood stroll. It literally did not occur to me that 3rd street was a very long street that went all the way downtown.

So I started driving and definitely noted I was going east for a very long time. But I had been willing to get in my car so I knew I needed to take advantage of this willingness and see it through. So I kept going. And going. And going. Until I finally arrived, at one of the scariest complexes imaginable. The way I remember it is that it was sort of like a Freddy Krueger-esque multi-building sort of camping site: you parked, walked down this dirt hill and there were various cabins and buildings dotted around. I followed the people who had been outside smoking into one of the buildings and sat down to experience the meeting.

I'm just going to say it right now: I was in the hood. At that point, I was very confused about 12-step, the process, all of it. I had been to one meeting, more like as a random field trip than anything else, when I was in high school in Marin, but this was very different. All I remember is this: the people were oh so kind to me. And they talked a lot about having different aliases. Apparently, the theme of the night was legal trouble and how to escape it, and among this group, changing your name and identity, getting new papers and documentation, was a popular method for dealing with it. I left armed with a lot of information about how to get a new identity and many more reasons to never come back to AA.

Then the time came when it occurred to me that I was willing again and so I asked a sober friend if he would take me, admitting to him that I was really scared. He promised that I didn't need to do anything but sit there next to him—no one would make me talk or do a thing. And he was right. Until the end of the meeting when, randomly, the secretary turned to me and handed over a laminated sheet. "Can you read the prayer?" he asked.

Whaa? I looked at my friend. He'd promised this wouldn't happen! And praying—this was worse than talking! WTF! My friend's face was blank. I wanted him to yell at the horrible man who'd handed me the laminated sheet and explain that he shouldn't hoist alarming tasks on someone who was just there auditing but my friend just shrugged. With all 100 or so people from the meeting looking at me, I handed the prayer back to the secretary.

"No" was all I said.

This is something I have never, in the God knows how many meetings I've been to over the past 18 years, seen someone do.

And then there was my final visit before I ended up in rehab. This time a guy I was dating told me I had a problem and needed to deal with it. I had another sober friend, a girl I'd helped arrange an intervention on because I'm a hypocrite of the highest order, and as a result of this intervention (which I remember arranging while experiencing coke drip), our relationship was strained. But I asked her to take me to a meeting and she agreed.

The meeting was cool. I heard some stuff that I thought might really help her but at that point I was certain that I was strictly a cocaine addict—that is, someone who could drink whatever she wanted—and so I decided to tune out anything that had to do with abstaining from alcohol. After the meeting, my friend took me to fellowship with her best friend from the program, and over that meal, I proceeded to explain to the two of them why it was different for me than it was for them and I could continue to drink while doing AA. Apparently, the next day, my friend's friend told her, and she told me, that I was an incredibly triggering person to be around because my denial reminded her so much of her and she was too much of a newcomer herself to be around me.

After that, I gave up on AA. At least until I went to rehab, was put in a druggie buggy and driven there. The first meeting we were taken to was creep central—it was in some run down small, dank room and there were only two other people there in addition to our group. They shared some creepy shit, the details of which I don't remember. But after the meeting, one of my new rehab friends turned to me and said, "Those were some weird ass shares." It was the first time I'd heard the word share used as a noun and for some reason, that delighted me. I suddenly felt like I understood the language, the code I'd imagined existed back when I tried to make the guy at John and Pete's Liquor Store admit that there was something I was supposed to say to be allowed into the meeting. And I felt a connection with the girl from rehab who said it, a connection that somehow bridged a gap I hadn't been able to bridge during my previous visits to 12-step.

I was probably just ready to get sober. Still, it was nice to know I was right: those were some weird ass shares. And that was okay.

Part 2
WHAT HAPPENED

My Four-Legged Interventionist

After an all-night binge, I had the habit of spontaneously deciding to take drastic action—which is how I ended up with two cats. I didn't know that one of them would end up saving my life.

When I was doing nothing but cocaine, I couldn't seem to look at my life and admit that a drug like cocaine wasn't something I should do. Because at this point, it—my partying life—felt like all I really had. So instead I'd do a more extreme version of the behavior of a girl who, depressed by a break-up, decides to spontaneously get her hair chopped off. The message that seemed to be going from my heart to my head was: do something drastic and you'll feel better!

My strategy was: wake up and get a tattoo. That's how I ended up with four tattoos in two months, when I'd never had a tattoo in my life.

I needed another strategy.

As any woman who's ever gotten a sudden bob or pixie cut after a tragic breakup knows, doing something that will radically alter your life in an attempt to avoid your feelings doesn't work. But I was in denial about most things back then and one night, passed out in a bed with one of my best female friends and a wannabe country singer we had both fooled around with before, it occurred to me what radical thing I could do that would help me feel better: I could get a cat. The guy—in between trying (and failing) to convince us to have a threesome and trying (and failing) to play us Willie Nelson songs on his guitar—kept complaining that someone had thrown his cat in the pool. He lived in an enormous Hollywood Hills mansion with a bunch of other guys and people were always partying until all hours of the night, which means that a cat being thrown in a pool wasn't a wholly outlandish occurrence.

My life felt so empty then—I was unemployed, writing screenplays no one cared about and drowning my feelings out with chemicals at every opportunity. And every time I heard the wannabe country western singer say the words "my cat" and "the pool," they sounded increasingly solid—like emblems of a life that had its feet firmly planted in the ground. Property, pools, pets...I recall thinking that those things sounded like evidence of a life, something that I, as a member of the walking dead, didn't have. And I wanted a life, or at least evidence of one. And since I wasn't likely to get a pool or substantial property anytime soon, I latched onto the most attainable-sounding item on the list the wanna-be country singer had unknowingly drawn for me.

A cat.

I didn't ask myself if I was ready for the responsibility. I didn't consider the fact that I'd unwittingly killed every plant I'd ever had. I don't remember thinking it through much at all. Instead, like the heartbroken girl sitting in the hairdresser's chair, I just sort of assumed that a little boy or girl kitten would give me a raison d'être.

Shortly after the idea occurred to me—it may have been the next day or the next year, it's impossible for me to figure out what happened when during those lost years—I found myself at a vet's office in West Hollywood where a cat that belonged to one of the vets had given birth. Again, I didn't consider much—or anything. I just played around with a litter of male orange tabbies—nearly all orange tabbies were male, the kindly vet told me—and took what I thought was the cutest one.

Just how out of it was I during those dark years? Well, when I took my cat—who by that point I'd named Toby—back to the vet a few months later to have him fixed, I was informed by the bemused vet that he was, in fact, a she.

"Are you serious?" I responded, humiliated. The truth is that I'd never really looked: I'd been told that he was a guy and it didn't occur to me to confirm. And by then, it seemed too late to change her name so I reasoned that Toby—like Sam, like Erin, like Chris—could easily be a girl's name.

I guess you could say my cat mom priorities were askew. It never occurred to me to, say, teach Toby that it wasn't appropriate to jump on the kitchen table when food was being served or to even be too vehement about stopping her from scratching the couch. Sure, I'd yell a half-hearted, "Toby—stop!" when I heard my furniture being ripped to shreds, but I never tried any of the techniques

I'd heard about, like spraying her with a water bottle whenever she did it, because that just sounded like too much trouble and besides, how was I supposed to figure out, in the increasingly foggy state I was living in, where one even got an empty spray canister? By the time I happened across a spray canister at the drug store, it felt like it was too late to bother starting.

It makes me sad for Toby when I think about the chaos that surrounded her early years. Because, as my drug problem grew worse, I began having more and more crazy, chain-smoking people around. I'd throw script readings, fondue parties, Truth or Dare games and just regular old parties but increasingly, all of those gatherings began to serve only one purpose: to gather together a group of people who enjoyed doing cocaine. The more coke I did, the more random the friends became until it was just essentially a circle of people who had nothing in common besides a shared desire to snort illegal chopped-up powder up their nostrils through dollar bills. Essentially, if you lived in West Hollywood and had a coke habit back then, you probably had a key to my apartment.

And sure, we'd pay attention to Toby when we weren't snorting lines or fixing each other's makeup or taking Polaroid photos that we were sure at the time made us look incredibly glamorous. But usually we just chain-smoked and got jittery and weird. There's a photo I have from those days that just breaks my heart—a guy whose name I still remember and a girl whose name I don't, each holding a lit cigarette, each looking wasted, sitting on my couch with a wide-eyed and scared-looking Toby behind them.

Alas, things got even worse for Toby during the final stage of my drug use—when even the fellow coke addicts weren't coming around anymore and it was just me and my cocaine. I'd spend several days in a row awake and wired, trying to write screenplays, chain-smoking and chugging alcohol whenever I felt like I needed to come down, and I'd break those frantic jags up with bouts of Ambien-influenced, sleep-of-the-dead slumber. I became more panicky than a cat—jumping at every noise, convinced that whatever I heard was the sound of Them coming for me (though I never seemed clear on who, exactly, They were). I essentially gave Toby—and myself—whatever's the opposite of a safe, serene environment.

After I'd had Toby about a year, I decided to get Lilly. Again, this was not well thought out—or thought out at all. I simply woke up one morning and wondered what the point of it all was. My life was virtually empty—I'd burned through all my friends, I'd stopped returning my parents' calls and I had been depressed for so long that I forgot I was actually depressed, I just thought life was one long, arduous, sad slog. Toby clearly hadn't saved me and I still couldn't seem to consider what really could. And so I decided that I'd just get another cat.

I ended up at a pet store in Mar Vista. Again, I didn't have a cat selection method. I just remember that was a litter of thick, grey-haired kittens of no particular breed and I picked one. I do recall having her checked out by a male vet who worked at the pet store because I remember thinking that he was reasonably young and handsome and I fantasized that he would save me somehow.

While he didn't—I never saw him again and couldn't pick him out of a two-man lineup today—Lilly may have.

I don't want to be dramatic. I am not going to claim my kitten made me see that I didn't need to slowly kill myself anymore. But from the beginning, Lilly was undeniably, unbelievably special. Even my cocaine-addled brain could see that. For one, her fur was far softer than anything I'd ever felt in my life: it's what I imagine the richest, most succulent velvets in the world must feel like. But it's also just—well, her. Yes, she's beautiful, with huge green eyes and what feels like pounds of thick grey fur, but it's more than that. Cats are, by their very nature, jittery, scared and a bit skeptical. Lilly's the opposite: there's no lap she won't jump on, no person she won't deluge with kisses, no front door she won't race to when she hears a doorbell, no obstruction she won't climb. And she somehow manages to be amusing—to go about her courageous adventures with a "Hey, look at me" energy that is legitimately, laugh-out-loud funny. "I normally hate cats," many a dog-lover has told me. "That cat is special." Or: "That cat is different." Or even, in the case of one guy I remember getting really stoned with back in the day: "That cat is sexy." (When I was high, I thought it was the most accurate description in the world. Only later did it seem creepy.) She is, I've been told by many of those people, a dog trapped in a cat's body.

And it's just a fact that a few weeks after this sweet little furball came into my life, I'd simply had enough of the late, jittery nights and realized I couldn't bear the loneliness and depression I was living with any longer.

Maybe she was giving me one of her nine lives. Maybe I was just ready. All I know for sure is that I haven't needed another cat since she came along. And, thank God, I haven't needed another tattoo, either.

I Wasn't a Pill Head
But Boy, I Liked Pills

While cocaine was my main man, I definitely cheated with pills.

Placing a pill in my mouth and washing it down with water is probably as natural to me as breathing. You could actually argue that it's *more* natural, because I've been told when I've been worked up about something, "Just breathe," and have needed absolutely no help at all with my pill taking.

I do it without thinking; one morning a few years ago, I took my regular slew of vitamins, forgot I did it and five minutes later, took the whole batch again. I only realized what I'd done when I went shopping and almost passed out in a store from, I guess, some sort of a supplement OD.

My first memory of taking a pill is when I was about 10, had a cold and my dad gave me Actifed. I remember it perfectly—particularly the glorious feeling of sinking against the cushions as if I'd just had chloroform put over my mouth.

From Actifed! Ah, the sweet low tolerance of youth.

I've always loved anything that made me pass out. Drinking was good for that at first but it had this unfortunate drawback of making me wake up insanely early the next morning, cursing the sunlight streaming in the window, even in a dark room.

And so Ambien was a natural for me. Back in the 90s, no one talked about Ambien. There were no media stories about how it makes you shove Thin Mints down your gullet without you remembering. No one discussed how they were scamming their doctors to get extra Ambien.

But I needed a scam because I was racing through the Ambien I was being prescribed. See, I was supposed to be cutting the pills into quarters only if I couldn't sleep and instead I was automatically taking four whole pills every night. Or at least I was for a while. Then I was taking five. And then six. Tolerance and Ambien go horribly together.

And so I came up with a lie for my doctor. It was pretty simple.

This was it: "I went to Palm Springs and left my pill bottle there."

Yep, that was it—the old "I lost the bottle" lie. Since my grandmother lived in Palm Springs, this didn't seem like too outrageous of a lie. After all, it *could* have happened.

But I also altered the story sometimes.

Sometimes it was "I went to San Francisco and left my pill bottle there."

Or: "I went to Arizona and left my pill bottle there."

I always kept the places I was allegedly leaving the pill bottle relatively close, possibly because this made it seem like less of a lie; by the time I was making these claims, I was barely leaving my apartment, let alone the city. Going to that shrink was as close as I was getting to travel.

For a while, he bought it. Then one day he told me he couldn't see me anymore and I "probably knew why." He didn't mention 12-step or rehab but I wouldn't have listened to him if he had.

Ever resourceful, I had other ways to get pills after the doc cut-off. California is, after all, quite close to Mexico. And so I went to Baja with a friend who made these sojourns regularly and I told the person behind the counter at the Pharmacia that I was anxious—three simple words and I walked away with sheets of pills, including Ambien, Xanax and Valium. Have you ever seen a sheet of pills? I felt so exalted by the acquisition that when I got home, I handed them out to friends like I was Pablo Escobar.

They didn't last long. I cursed myself for having been so generous.

When I got sober, I was more than willing to admit that my relationship with cocaine was unmanageable but balked when I was told that I also seemed to be addicted to pills. Didn't these people understand that I suffered from insomnia? They didn't. Or they did but they didn't much care. I was put on a medication called Trazodone, an SSRI that's also used as a sleeping aid.

Trazodone did the trick for many years but while SSRIs are technically not addictive, my emotional attachment to them was severe.

One time I went to Jamaica and left my bottle of Trazodone on the plane (clear karmic payback for those doctor lies years before). I was staying in a town called Treasure Beach, which was 80 miles west of Kingston. Eighty miles. Which means we drove for two hours to get from the airport to the hotel and it was only when I got there that I realized what I'd done.

Let me clarify that I do not speak patois. Let me also clarify that the hotel where we were staying, which was really more of a beach shack then a hotel, had no phone that guests could use. And this was way before I had a cell that worked internationally.

In a panic, I paid someone at the hotel to take me to "town" to find something, anything, I could use as a sleeping aid. We walked up and down the desolate strip that was considered town, and while I was offered "ganja" from extremely friendly drug dealers literally every step I took (and even cocaine from some dealers clearly branching out from the norm there), the strongest thing I could buy at the one pharmacy/supermarket was cold medicine.

Alas, my tolerance wasn't what it was at 10.

I returned to the hotel determined to get my bottle of pills back and so I convinced the people at the hotel to let me use the house phone to call the Kingston airport. I called that airport more times than I can count and tried to communicate what I needed to many people before ultimately giving up. It was actually more effort than I'd put into scoring drugs as an active addict.

Then, my second day there, a man drove up in a rickety car and crazily, amazingly, handed the bottle of Trazodone over. The people at the hotel told me, in patois-English (my ability to understand improved immeasurably during my drug seeking 24 hours), that it was absolutely impossible that I'd managed to convince someone to look for the bottle on the plane, let alone find it, let alone drive it 80 miles.

Clearly, despite living in the ganja capital of the world, these people didn't understand the determination of drug addicts—a skill that apparently doesn't disappear just because you get sober.

Many years into taking it, I decided to try to get off Trazodone. That's when I made an amazing discovery: I may *not* have trouble sleeping after all. What I have more than insomnia is anxiety that I will have insomnia. And so now I cut my Traz into quarters and then take one of them only if I feel like I may be anxious about sleeping that night. I keep an Excel spreadsheet and if I take one of those quarter pills, I mark it on the sheet. I fully realize this is insane; my shrink told me a quarter of a pill is a complete placebo. My ex would tell me, when he'd find little baggies filled with cut-up Trazodone in random drawers at his place, that I was a crazy person—and also that I talked about sleep more than anyone he'd ever met. But those crazy little cut up non pills serve as my security blanket and well, as evidenced by the fact that I just told you this story, I find sharing about sleep fascinating. Sobriety, in other words, does not guarantee sanity.

Though I've found that it does help with sleep. Eventually.

Dating as a Newcomer

When you have been on this planet for nearly three decades, you do not like to be told that you are insane. You have, after all, made it very far for an insane person. Or have you? You ended up in rehab so there's that. But clearly you know stuff. Right? And so when the people you meet start telling you that you aren't capable of making any good decisions so you best hold off on that whole concept for a good year and my God you shouldn't be dating because you'll be choosing with a broken picker, you are rightfully offended.

I had spent the previous three years holed up in my West Hollywood apartment with only cats and gay men for company. Suddenly I was back among the living, forming sentences that didn't involve asking people to pass the mirror and some of these conversations were with members of the opposite sex. Not date? I was finally *ready* to date!

I found my first conquest in my second week of sobriety. It was a guy—let's call him David—I'd met years before, out in LA, and while I'd been attracted to him then and given him my number, I was completely flummoxed when he called and asked me out—not by the fact that he was asking me out but by what in God's name we would do on a date. This guy was *sober*. Would we go to the beach? For some reason, that was the only thing I could think of that two people could do on a date that didn't involve alcohol, and the beach is a good 40-minute drive and very cold at night (a daytime sober date was out of the question) and so I never returned his call.

I remembered him though and so, when I was at a big Friday night meeting and saw him standing in line waiting to thank the speaker, I was thrilled. There he was—the person who was going to help me forget all about the incredible discomfort I was feeling, the one who was going to distract me from the fact that I was making the scariest change of my life, the guy who would be by my side at meetings so I wouldn't have to walk in alone. I didn't see any of this consciously, of course. I just saw him, thought, "Oh he's cute," then "Oh I know him," then, "Oh he asked me out once" and then I was standing next to him and explaining how incredibly sober I was.

"That's great!" he enthused. "How long?"

"Two weeks," I responded, quite proud.

"Wow," he said. "Good job." Or something like that. I don't remember what he said because I was too busy focusing on my next words, which were, "Why don't we go out now?"

"Whaaa?" he asked. "Uh, I…we can't. I'm 10 years sober. You're…"

"Also sober," I said. "Makes a lot more sense than us going out before. Take my number," I insisted. He did.

I can't remember the details of how this played out but somehow he ended up coming over to my place one night soon after. I don't recall much about it except that we made out, that he told me he'd worked in an insane asylum and that I had a notebook that had that "Dance like no one's watching" expression on the front and I thought the notebook was super cheesy but he picked it up and said, "That's the most beautiful thing I ever heard." I figured we were starting our relationship. But then he didn't call me afterwards.

I became obsessed with him. This was pre-Facebook and pre-texting, meaning there were very few ways to act on an obsession. All you could do was bore your friends silly and make up scenarios in your head about what could have made everything go so terribly wrong. I couldn't figure it out; he'd liked me when I was a coke-addled mess. Now that I was so sober and sane and together, he didn't?

They say that romantic obsessions are never about the person you're obsessed with. Instead, the person you're obsessed with is triggering something in you and even though you're convinced it's their soul or face or body that has its hook in you, really it has nothing to do with them. I realized this a few weeks later when I forgot all about David and stumbled across my new obsession. Let's call him Pete.

To me, Pete was the king of AA. He was sober a long time, the secretary of a super cool meeting, sponsored celebrities and everything he said was hilarious. After I heard him speak at a meeting one morning, I decided he would be my boyfriend. I set about making this happen by grabbing the secretary of the meeting a few days later.

"I really, really, really like Pete," I told him.

"I get it," he responded. "I can't tell you the number of girls I thought I was in love with when I was new."

I was wildly offended. He was writing off my having *fallen in love at first sight* as some crazy newcomer thing?! I realized this guy was not going to do the set up I'd envisioned him offering to do. "So where does Pete go to meetings?"

He mentioned a few and I made it my mission to go there. And though I don't remember the details, I know I was able to work something out because Pete and I ended up on a date at a now-long-gone café. I remember that we made out. I remember that I randomly had a meeting at VH1 the next morning to talk about doing on-air appearances for them. I remember that I, fresh in the glow of having made out with my obsession, spent much of the meeting asking them if they were aware of this amazing new talent on the horizon. Pete, you see, was an aspiring comic; I'd been to some of his sparsely attended shows. The VH1 executives were, to say the least, not aware of him but thanked me for the info. I didn't get on-air at VH1 but was thrilled that I'd been able to get my new boyfriend on their radar.

Pete did not call.

A week or so later, when I realized that Pete was not going to call, I decided that I hated him and would let him know that in what I thought was the most effective way possible: by glaring at him whenever I saw him at meetings. This scared him enough that he avoided me for the most part—until the day a few months later when I was standing on the steps outside another meeting and he made the approach.

"Hey, Anna," he said. I glared. "I just wanted to thank you," he persevered. "I had a great meeting at VH1 last week and they told me they got my name through you. That was really cool of you." Now I glared—and hated both of us.

I moved on to many more obsessions over the years, never really understanding—until the pain got so great that I had to—that I was just doing "same person, new face" dating.

In case I ever need a reminder, I conveniently still see both David and Peter in meetings. They are each about 30 years sober and are both still dating newcomers.

When I was about three years sober, I started running into David at meetings a lot. One of those times, he asked me out. "We went out," I reminded him. "You blew me off!"

"You were new!" he responded. "I couldn't date you!"

"So making out with me and not calling me was okay but dating me was wrong?" I asked.

He paused. "Yeah," he finally said.

I went out with him about six years later, when I ran into him and he asked me out again. He was 20 minutes late to pick me up for a movie we went to see at Mann's Chinese. Now let me pause and say that any date that has and will ever take place at Mann's Chinese is doomed because it's the most annoying place on earth. It is especially annoying when you are 20 minutes late to a movie and your date says it's your fault because this plan had been made over Facebook and he'd asked for your number during the exchange and you hadn't given it to him and if he'd had it, he could have called you on the way to tell you he was late and the two of you could have made a plan to see another movie. It is even more annoying when your date hoovers the popcorn even though you told him you like to eat an entire popcorn so if he thinks he might want some, he should buy his own. Despite this, despite my complete silence on the drive home, David parked his car in front of my house. "I'm coming in, right?" he said.

"Wrong," I answered. I was 10 years sober then. My picker wasn't working perfectly but it was working better.

Making Amends Was Everything I Least Expected

Ah, amends. Even before you're sober, you hear about them. Sober people, I knew since long before I got sober myself, were always out there apologizing.

That doesn't mean I understood the concept. For instance, if you'd asked me then if apologizing and making amends were the same thing, I'd have sworn that they were. I had no experience, yet, of making things right with someone I'd wronged—let alone making things right in a way that might stop me from repeating whatever it was I'd done in the first place.

By the time I got to my Ninth Step, I'd picked up a few things. Probably the most important one was that I didn't have to play the victim anymore. My Fourth and Fifth steps had showed me that *I* had played a major part in all my resentments—a realization that I found liberating. Steps Six, Seven and Eight had gotten me ready to make my amends. And while I was certainly nervous about getting started on what I then thought of as my apology tour, I was also excited.

I figured I'd knock out the "easy" ones first: one to Lauren and another to Clay, both former party pals. In each case I'd done something gossipy and mean-spirited but not atrocious, so I figured these amends would be simple. These people weren't, after all, family members who were likely to make the experience traumatizing, or exes whom I dreaded to contact at all. They were just people I'd once spent a lot of time around but didn't really have anything in common with anymore. Easy, right?

I called Lauren first (this was in the days before Caller ID or the demise of landlines):

"Lauren? Hey, it's Anna."

Long pause.

"Hey, Anna."

"So listen. I'm calling because—"

"Oh, God, don't tell me this is one of those 'amends' type of calls. I just—"

"Please let me—"

"Look, I heard you're sober and that's great. But this just isn't something I'm up for."

Click.

I sat there listening to the dial tone. In all the amends scenarios I'd mentally concocted, having someone—let alone the first person I reached out to—not be willing to hear what I had to say had never occurred to me. I'd read in the Big Book that we had to be willing to go to people we feared might throw us out of their offices, but I'd never read anything about how to handle the people who wouldn't even take the call to set up the meeting. Still, what could I do—call her back, tell her it was about something else and sneak an amends in? My sponsor told me to move on, so I did.

To Clay. Who, well, never called me back. I didn't realize he wasn't ever planning to call me back until a week or so after I'd left a voicemail, when our mutual friend told me. "He doesn't like to revisit the past," the friend explained. "He said you don't need to apologize for anything."

This wasn't how I'd imagined it going. I'd heard other people share about how they'd suddenly find themselves running into the very person they'd been planning to make amends to that day. Why was the opposite happening to me?

But I moved on. I had to. And I continued to find the process nothing like I expected it to be.

In general, it seemed like the people I thought weren't going to be amenable to even meeting up welcomed me warmly. Those I thought would forgive me right away, meanwhile, were dismissive or indifferent. But one thing remained predictable: The amends that I was so terrified to make that I shook with terror or sobbed at the thought were always the most rewarding of all.

Take, for instance, the ex I'd never gotten over. I called him up one evening when I was about five years sober and told him how sorry I was for destroying our relationship, for every cruel thing I'd uttered and each horrible mistake I'd made when we were together. But rather than lay into me as I expected, he said he was glad to hear from me, that it helped him make sense of his past, that he was happy I was sober and doing well. But, he added, I was blaming myself too much; he'd played just as big a part in what had gone wrong between us as I had. The conversation was more honest, painful and beautiful than any we'd had the entire time we lived together. I hung up feeling about 20 pounds lighter. I was finally free of an idea I hadn't even realized I'd been clinging to—that I'd been a monster and he my innocent victim.

Then there was the time I met up with a friend I'd known since I was 12 but had fallen out with in my 20s. We went on a hike and I told her how sorry I was for the way I'd behaved the last time we'd spoken, five or so years earlier. It turned out she was in a 12-step program too—so she actually made amends to me right after I made them to her. By the time we got to the bottom of the canyon, we'd re-launched our friendship—on new, healthier terms.

I was promised miracles and they came—but never how or when I expected them.

Take my financial amends. The first debt that I owed was to my college roommate, for the time I'd borrowed her car in sophomore year and then acted surprised when I saw the dent. I explained to her that I'd actually crashed into something when drunk and lied to her, and that I wanted to reimburse her for the damages. But she wouldn't hear of it.

For my next financial amends, I decided to just go ahead and send a check. It was to a girl I'd lived with when I first moved to New York after college, a girl who'd moved out of our crappy, railroad-style place without notice one Thanksgiving weekend when I was out of town. It was a shitty thing to do, of course. But it didn't make it right for me to charge up the phone bill in her name as high as I could, and then not respond when she asked me to reimburse her. So I tracked down her address and mailed a check and a card, apologizing for the phone bill as well as for being—well, the kind of roommate who would inspire someone to move out over Thanksgiving weekend without notice.

She sent the check back, along with a note that said, essentially, that she was doing very well, that she had a husband, five kids and a thriving career as a chiropractor, and that if I felt so bad about my behavior, then I should donate the money to a good cause since she didn't need my charity.

Like I said, not what I expected. But even that one allowed me to live with a little more freedom.

Some amends haven't involved contacting people at all. Glenn, a roommate I'd lived with in New York, started off cool as could be but slowly revealed himself to be crazy—a guy who'd lock my cats away when I was out and call the landlord when I had friends from AA over, saying that he was "scared for his life" because there were "homeless alcoholics" around. (To say I've had bad luck with New York roommates would be an understatement.)

Though I ended up moving out and getting away from him entirely, I found myself still resenting him months later. I had done plenty wrong in our relationship, but trying to make amends to him was something I couldn't imagine—not when he'd done things to me that I couldn't imagine getting over. I decided to make a "living amends" by trying to be kind and gracious in my life—the opposite of how I'd been toward him at the end. But that didn't stop me from resenting him. So, at my sponsor's suggestion, I committed to praying for him for 90 days—specifically for him to get everything he wanted and for me to have empathy for the fact that he'd been doing the best he could. I did it for those three months, never feeling any differently about him but staying committed to the process because my sponsor kept asking me about it. I thought it was silly: I never felt any differently about Glenn.

Until the day, months after I'd stopped praying for him, that I met a gay guy who asked me if I knew anyone great to set him up with and I found myself answering, without thinking, "Yes! I know this amazing guy named Glenn."

Glenn! As in: the guy I hated. *Had* hated, apparently.

Those days and weeks and months of asking an entity I didn't even understand to give Glenn what he wanted had apparently granted me the empathy to see that he only hurt me because of the pain he was in himself. And this had relieved me of my resentment, without me even realizing. It was surreal. (And no, I didn't set the two guys up—I had no interest in ever talking to Glenn again—but the space he'd been taking up in my head was cleared.)

I still do things I need to make amends for. Sometimes I make them right away and sometimes not for a long time. But I've found that time works in surprising ways when it comes to these things. Consider, for instance, what happened with Clay—the guy who wouldn't call me back when I first started making my amends. Years had passed—so many years that he'd forgotten I'd ever said or done anything hurtful to him—when I ran into him one evening outside the gym. He told me that he'd just gotten an offer to sell a book of poetry, then asked if I'd be willing to look over the contract the publisher was asking him to sign.

I said I'd be happy to, and we met up a few days later, when I looked over his contract and gave him the best advice I could. Then I told him how sorry I was about the hurtful thing I'd done so many years before. I still remember how shocked his bright blue eyes looked when they jumped from the contract pages to meet mine. Then they filled with tears. Turns out, this thing I'd done that was "just" gossipy and mean-spirited had actually been something I needed to make right. And the guy who didn't like to "revisit the past," who'd told a friend I didn't have to apologize for anything, ended up accepting my apology lovingly, giving me one more opportunity to chip away at the guilt and shame I didn't want to walk around with anymore. He just hadn't been able to do it on my time schedule.

Lauren still hasn't surfaced. But that's not to say that she won't.

Nobody Believes Me When I Tell Them I Used to Smoke Two Packs a Day

When I tell people that I used to smoke two packs of cigarettes a day, they look at me askance—and I don't blame them. Do you know how hard it is to smoke two packs of cigarettes a day? That's 40 f-ing smokes. You have to wake up and do it before you do anything else. It has to be the last thing you do before you fall asleep, which can be dangerous. And you have to focus on it all day long, navigating your way through numerous situations where smoking isn't allowed and planning it like you're going on a combat mission—which essentially you are. That's a full-time job. Conveniently, for many years, including the time in my life when I was smoking two packs a day, I was remarkably unemployed.

A lot of kids, or at least kids like me, fall into smoking. But I wonder how many of them remember driving onto the freeway at the age of 16, pushing the lighter in, lighting one of their mom's Merit Ultra Lights, inhaling when they looked in the rearview mirror and saying to themselves, "When I grow up, I'm going to be a smoker. Like a real one. Not one who just steals Merit Ultra Lights from her mom's purse."

My dreams came true—and I didn't even have to make it far into adulthood for it to happen, either. I went from casual smoker to hard core smoker during the spring break of my freshman year of college when my dance class went to New York to perform with a professional troupe. The irony of this was not lost on me. I was in a sense a professional athlete and in another sense a professional smoker. I remember feeling very pleased with myself as I trudged around Manhattan smoking.

And then it was, as they say, off to the races. For the next decade, every meal or sexual experience I had was punctuated with a cigarette—or two. I was actually fond of saying that I only ate and had sex so that I could enjoy the cigarette after. I smoked through jobs, boyfriends, car rides and workouts. Oh yeah did I mention I've always been a hardcore exerciser, even when I smoked? Even during the two-pack a day days. When I lived in England my junior year in college and got around Cambridge on a bicycle, I smoked the whole time I rode. I justified this because I didn't have a car and I always smoked while driving. When I returned to the States, I tried to cut down on smoking; one of my methods was that I had a very strict rule with myself that I wouldn't smoke once I was in my workout clothes. I would try putting on my workout clothes early in the day to prevent myself from becoming a human chimney, but it was too easy to change clothes so that stopped working.

The summer between my junior and senior years, however, the universe gave me a gift—in the form of tonsillitis that wouldn't go away. As it turns out, tonsillitis doesn't go away when you take

NOBODY BELIEVES ME

penicillin but drink and smoke the whole
to-back bouts of it, my Ear, Nose and Throa
was essentially my age and who looked like he
sillectomy in his life—told me my tonsils had to c

Because I only watched one TV show as a kid and I h.
episode a minimum of 20 times, I only thought of Cinc
ol Brady eating lots of ice cream after their twin tonsillect. Jies on *The Brady Bunch*. I thought it sounded kind of fun.

I didn't mention to my doctor that my body had been accustomed to smoking two packs of cigarettes a day but he did mention to me that if you took tonsils out when a person was older (19 is considered older in the tonsil world), there could be some complications. He didn't go into specifics. And he didn't need to because I got to live the complications first hand when, a few days after the surgery, one of the sutures in my throat split and I started coughing up blood. See, something I hadn't factored in is that when you are smoking two packs of cigarettes a day and then you suddenly stop, you are not only nicotine-deprived but also so filled with phlegm that you do nothing but cough.

And if there's anything that's going to break a throat suture, it's, well, coughing.

My mom, who's coffee-obsessed to a degree that she drinks coffee while she meditates, always had to-go pint coffee cups on hand for when she needed to leave the house while imbibing. This is how I know that I coughed up more than a pint of blood that day. With blood clots pouring out of my throat and into those handy pint cups, my mom drove me to the hospital where the ENT shot Novocain down my throat and tried to stop a broken suture he couldn't see because it was too far down my throat. Anyone who hasn't gagged by a suture closing stick while swallowing Novocain, consider yourself lucky.

My point in telling you this grotesque story is that the aftermath of this incident meant that I couldn't eat, let alone smoke, for over three weeks. I was three weeks off the smokes! The three hardest weeks were handled! I went back to college my senior year determined not to smoke, clutching this cigarette pencil whenever I had the urge and self-righteously announcing, whenever someone asked me if they could bum a smoke, that I had quit.

That lasted less than a week. Back to the smokes I went, with all the determination of someone who hadn't been coughing up pints of blood mere weeks before.

Smoking saw me through the lowest points of my drug addiction because Camel Lights mix better with cocaine than peanut butter does with jelly. And then they saw me through rehab and early sobriety. Smoking after meetings became my new smoking after doing coke in the bathroom.

And then something weird happened. I had dinner with a woman after a meeting one night and when she found out I smoked, she turned to me and earnestly asked, "Honey, why are you putting a smoke screen between you and God?" Something happened inside of me when she asked but something more happened when she told me that I should meet her at a Nicotine Anonymous meeting the next night, since the guy I'd told her I had a mad crush on also went.

I had no intention of quitting smoking. I just wanted to be around that dude. But I didn't want to show up at the meeting reeking of cigarettes and so I only had a few smokes the next day and then met her at the meeting that night. I sat in between her and the guy.

I listened to the speaker. And then the guy asked me if I wanted to go to coffee and talk about how much we were craving cigarettes.

He really thought I was doing this quitting thing! It made him want to bond with me! How could I tell him I didn't really want to quit but had just wanted to be somewhere that he was guaranteed to be?

"Oh, yes," I answered. "I need to talk about the cravings."

And so he and I had coffee and during that coffee he told me he had been in love with his cousin—not like a cousin by marriage or something but actual cousin—and my crush on him evaporated instantly. But by then, I hadn't smoked since noon that day. It was 8:30 pm. I hadn't gone that many hours without a cigarette, aside from when I was asleep, in years. I decided to see what would happen if I didn't smoke for the rest of the night.

Here's what happened: the next morning, really just as an experiment, I decided to see what would happen if I tried to keep this whole not smoking thing going. And I did. I haven't smoked since. That was July 19th, 2000.

Just because I stopped then doesn't mean it was easy or problem-free. It was a nightmare; I was so delirious during my withdrawal that I would walk into, say, a drug store with the intention of buying toothpaste and walk out holding a Danish that had been in a package there since, seemingly, the 70s. I went back to that Nicotine Anonymous meeting and the one time the speaker didn't call on me to share, I went up afterwards and yelled at her for not understanding that NEWCOMERS NEED TO SHARE. She told me to keep coming back and I cried. You get it—I was a mess.

Now I've become that nightmare ex-smoker, the one who holds her nose when she walks by groups of people smoking on the street and who says, if someone smoking a cigarette tries to hug her, "I'm sorry—I don't hug people who are smoking." I don't know how or exactly when I transitioned from girl who automatically liked someone if they were a smoker to the most sanctimonious ex-smoker in the country but I do know this: the 16-year-old me would be ashamed.

Babysitting (with) a Movie Star

There are benefits of sobriety that Bill W. never could have predicted—particularly if you live in LA.

I learned one of them the day that a bunch of us were sitting in a coffee shop after a meeting and one of the biggest movie stars in the world joined us.

The movie star had not been in the meeting but we all knew he was sober and was friends with one of the guys we were with. And so we all did the most logical thing: we pretended that we had absolutely no idea who he was.

After about a half hour of acting on my part that was at least as solid as some of the movie star's early work, he turned to me and asked if my friend and I wanted to join him at the pool of the hotel next door for a swim.

Pretending that this was a perfectly quotidian request, I responded, "Sure, let me just run home and grab my suit!" And I did.

As the day progressed, I almost convinced myself that it was perfectly normal to be hanging out with one of the world's biggest movie stars. And so when he casually announced that he had his kid that night and asked if the three of us wanted to come over while he babysat, it didn't even feel weird to shrug and say, "Sure, why not?"

And that's it: because my friend and the guy we were with had plans, I'd landed a date with the movie star.

When I arrived at his cavernous loft later that evening, he gave my lips a quick peck and gestured for me to follow him into his kitchen.

"What do you feel like doing?" he asked. "Want to take a walk on the beach?" He said this like I came over all the time and determining our nightly plans was simply part of our ritual.

Just then, a small dark-haired boy came barreling into the room and threw himself around the movie star's legs.

"Hey, you. What's up?" the movie star said, tousling the kid's hair. "Want to come walk with Daddy and his friend on the beach?"

The child gazed at me with wide eyes. "I'm Diego," he announced.

"I'm—"

"Anna," the movie star finished and I was both impressed by the movie star's ability to remember my name and horrified by how easily impressed I was.

"Hi, Anna." Diego scattered out from under his dad's arm and ran up to me. "Are you going to be spending the night?"

I didn't know what to say so I forced a laugh. The movie star smiled.

"Chill out, kid," he said affectionately. "Where's Sam?"

Diego yelled, "Sa-am!" and a towheaded kid came scampering into the room.

"Are we going out for pizza?" Sam asked the movie star. I longed to be as comfortable as these children.

The movie star didn't introduce me and I decided it wasn't worth getting offended over not officially meeting a prepubescent. "No, we're going to play ball on the beach," he said. "Right, Anna?"

Despite still being scarred by the memory of grammar school dodgeball, I tried to smile.

Maybe it was that his face was about as familiar to me as my own. Maybe it was that he was undeniably sexy. Or maybe I just hoped that a game of ball (football? baseball? who knew?) would calm my nerves ever so slightly. Running around on the beach with a couple of kids could maybe help me forget the fact that I was standing in the home of someone I'd had posters of my entire adolescence.

"We sure are," I said, tossing off the platform heels that I'd so carefully selected for this excursion. "Who's coming?"

And then I was on the beach, tossing an enormous beach ball toward Sam. He caught it, which made me feel enormously validated, and tossed it back. Next to us, the movie star and his son kicked a soccer ball back and forth.

"Bet you can't catch it if I throw it really high!" I yelled at Sam and tossed the ball up what I imagined was going to be hundreds of feet in the air only to have it fly about a foot up before flopping to the ground. Sam good-naturedly ran toward me to retrieve it.

"That was lame!" he yelled as he scooped the ball up and made his way back to where he was standing before.

I was trying to figure out if Sam knew I was faking interest in the impromptu beach ball game and obsessively wondering if my cavalier act was working as we played nonsensical ball games on the beach. Or did the movie star have so many different women over that the sight of a slightly uncomfortable, overly enthusiastic woman didn't even seem like a fact worth noting?

Then the movie star walked over to me and grabbed my hand. "I'm just trying to tire these guys out so they'll crash," he said, and his face cracked into one of his famous, beautiful smiles. "You're an angel for helping me out here."

"Are you kidding? I love it," I said, worrying that my voice sounded fake, even though, at the moment, I felt like I was telling the truth.

On the walk back to his place, we stopped for pizza. While the kids played arcade games, the movie star and I sat at a table waiting for the food.

Now, it's always been my firm belief that when two people are sitting together, it is the equal responsibility of both parties to contribute to the conversation. Of course, it usually happens naturally—one person says something or asks a question, the other responds, and conversation starts to just unfold.

But in this case, it didn't happen. I already knew where the movie star was from, how he'd been discovered, who he'd dated and that he dropped out of high school, so all the what-did-you-want-to-be-when-you-grew up, what-do-your-parents-do, what-did-you-major in types of questions—standard first date fare—felt like they would be silly and redundant.

Forcing a conversation about what was going on in the world would feel just that—forced—and I wasn't interested enough in food to start discussing the menu. I was, for one of the first times I could remember, at a complete and utter conversational loss.

And then I felt just the slightest glimmer of hope in him. He could ask me the typical first date questions, about what I did for a living or why I decided to get sober. Flooded with sudden optimism, I smiled at him. He smiled back and I assumed he was going to ask me something, but instead he took his index finger and tapped the table, then his other index finger and did the same thing. And, before I know it, he was doing some kind of impromptu drum solo on the table of the pizza place, clearly grooving to some wild beat inside his head.

As we walked back, however, communication picked up. At one point, he grabbed my hand to point out a shooting star and I couldn't help but see us as a stranger, or a camera, might. Back at his place, he stuck the kids in a media room watching a movie, and brought me into a living room, where we started kissing. I felt a million times more comfortable making out with him than I did making conversation with him.

Pretty soon we were lying down on the couch and he was on top of me. But as he started unbuttoning my jeans, I moved his hand away.

"I just don't feel comfortable going there right now," I whispered and he nodded, but a few seconds later, he went for the buttons again. I may have run right over here the minute he asked, and may have been grinding up against him despite the fact that he hadn't given me any indication that he was actually interested in anything about me, but I knew I'd feel badly about myself if I had sex with him. I reasoned that we might go out again and who knows, maybe even have a relationship, so the idea of having sex with him on our first only semi-date would therefore surely not be a good idea.

And so when he reached for my zipper again I said, "I just don't have sex with someone right away."

He furrowed his brow as if he were confused and it occurred to me that this may very well have been the first time he'd even heard of the concept of not jumping right into bed.

"You mean, you'd be into maybe going out again and fooling around a little more that time and then having it go from there?" he asked, and I nodded. "God, that sounds nice," he said, looking suddenly completely relaxed and I wondered why I'd allowed myself to be so intimidated by him earlier. He kissed me again, and then said, "Want to spend the night? We wouldn't have to do anything—we could just spoon."

I shook my head and he pouted somewhat adorably. "Are you sure?" he asked. "It would be so sweet—the kiddies are up in my bed."

I sat up suddenly, too surprised to worry about how I was probably killing the moment. "The kids are in your bed?" I asked.

"Sure." He smiled. "That's where Diego likes to sleep."

"And you want me to sleep there with all you guys?"

He nodded and smiled and I couldn't decide if I was a secret straitlaced conservative or if asking a girl you just met to spend the night in the same bed with your son and his friend was as crazy as I thought it was.

I left soon after and he texted me the next day asking if I wanted to go out again. We texted back and forth for a while before the whole thing petered out. Weeks later, rather than considering this a fun life experience, I actually managed to talk myself into feeling massively rejected by the movie star because he hadn't enthusiastically pursued me.

Shortly after that, I read in a magazine that he'd gotten married to a normal person—that is, a non-movie star. My alcoholic thinking kicked in again, reminding me that I was inferior to whomever this woman was.

But then I was saved by a single thought…How many table drum solos would this woman be enduring over the years? While I don't know the answer, I can happily say that I think my own number may be zero.

Even Sober, I Was a Nightmare Employee

I used to live by the credo that in order to have my respect, you had to earn my respect.

There are myriad reasons as to how and why I landed on that winner of a philosophy but the point is that for the majority of my life, I justified all kinds of egregious behavior with superiors under the conviction that I didn't need to respect people just because I was told to.

This is an excellent way to live if you'd like to alienate teachers and bosses. It is in turn a terrific way to wind up enraged because you didn't receive the grade you felt you deserved, not to mention unemployed.

I didn't antagonize all my teachers and bosses and actually had wonderful relationships with many of them. But if I felt someone who had authority over me didn't know what he or she was doing or didn't appreciate me in the way I deserved (or, worst of all, both), I adopted an I'll-show-'em mentality. You don't like me? Well, I'm going to show you that I don't like you. Oh, and I'll subtly point out whenever I can that I know more than you.

We probably don't need to discuss how many times I've been fired.

It was my conduct when I worked at *People* magazine in the 90s that really put me in the running for Employer's Biggest Nightmare. I've never behaved more alcoholically at a job, but I don't mean I was pounding Jim Beam at my desk and blowing coworkers under it.

No, what I was doing was far less sexy: I was so insecure about my ability to do the job that I acted like I knew everything. I basically drowned my inferiority complex in superiority without any idea that I was doing it. Oh also, I wasn't good at my job.

The work entailed covering events and doing profiles on celebrities. The event stories were a wash because my alcoholism had met something new and fell madly in love: premieres and award shows with open bars. I had my pen and paper but that pen got a little wobbly as the nights went on. More than once, a celebrity's publicist contacted the magazine to say that I'd misquoted them.

The profiles were also problematic because I mostly interviewed men and my main goal tended to be to try to make the subject fall in love with me rather than getting all the information I needed.

When my boss talked to me about the mistakes I was making, I'd get upset and essentially tell him to stop picking on me. One day, during one of those conversations, he asked me to pack up my stuff and leave for good.

I assumed I'd left all that bad employee behavior behind when I got sober. It certainly seemed like I had for my first few years in recovery. But what I failed to notice during that time is that I was writing books and articles—i.e., pretty much working for myself.

Then, when I was about 10 years sober, I took a job.

Let me say this in my own defense: I was good at it. I put an entire website together under the worst, most emotionally abusive site owner you can imagine. But as our 12-step literature says (and I'm paraphrasing), the shitty things people do to us aren't relevant because we're still responsible for what we do. I behaved horribly—took everything personally and raged right back—justifying it with the rationale that I wasn't as bad as my boss.

He eventually left and I thought my problems there were over. But by then he'd installed someone above me who I was convinced didn't know what he was doing. I see now that he did, of course—that's why he had the job. But my ego was on fire; I'd built the site up and then had my power usurped because of a decision a crazy man had made.

This was, of course, not my new boss' fault.

But you wouldn't know that from the way I treated him.

There were very few days when I didn't show in some creative new way that I thought I knew more than him. While passive aggression was my main mode of attack, I wasn't afraid to dip into active aggression either. By that time, the website had a new owner and I started talking to him about how much more capable I was than the current guy in charge and how unfair it was that he got to run things when I'd earned that right. The owner listened to me but didn't take any action. This frustrated me. So one day, when my boss had done something I found particularly irresponsible, I called the owner up and went off on him about it.

End result: I was fired and my boss was not.

I was 12 years sober. I had done countless inventories, made a plethora of amends, prayed for many character defects to be removed and grown exponentially as a human being since the gossip magazine days when I'd gotten shitfaced and misquoted Kenny G (yes, he was one of the celebrities who called up angry and yes, this was the 90s).

But I was still a nightmare employee.

I don't think I realized any of this, really, until I became an employer and had to contend with a few nightmare employees myself. That's when I discovered that it doesn't matter how talented or responsible someone is if you're in a constant battle with the person's ego.

Like many employers, I still have people I answer to and I don't always like what they tell me. In the beginning of this arrangement, I would complain to them when I felt justified and make excuses when they asked me to do something I didn't want to. And then one day it occurred to me how crazy it drove me when people working for me did those things. That's when I made a decision to always try to give a simple yes when I was asked to do something I didn't want to and just say I was sorry if I was informed I'd made a mistake.

Turns out, as self-help book-y as it sounds, showing respect for authority gave me respect for myself. I hadn't realized it but haranguing bosses until I got fired and telling myself I was just standing up for myself felt fucking awful—it epitomized the concept that resenting someone is like drinking poison and expecting the other person to die. Losing an argument, if you can call saying you're sorry and not making an excuse losing, actually feels like winning.

After a good year of stewing over what happened to me at my former job, I did an inventory and then made amends to the boss who'd tormented me and I'd tormented right back, the guy he installed above me and the final site owner. Even though I never heard back from one of them, the resentment I'd had—for all of them and myself—dissipated.

I'm not, of course, some bright shiny example of a worker bee. My ego gets involved and there's a lot I still have to learn about how to manage people. And I haven't cleaned up everything from my employment past.

Speaking of which, if you come across Kenny G, please tell him I'm sorry.

Networking in the Nuthouse

"I'm hot and you're hot," the message read. "Plus, I'm sober and you're sober."

This was a missive that appeared in my MySpace message box back when referencing MySpace didn't make you feel old. And look, I knew it was an incredibly douche-y introduction. But, my friends, you did not see the face (and body) that accompanied it. Since I can't do this justice in words, let me just say that it was enough to render the message both charming and clever.

Of course, I wrote back this beautiful stranger who was 3000 miles away. And of course, he responded to that. And so, before you knew it, we were engaged in the type of relationship addicts excel in—fantasy and artifice masquerading as a true connection with illusion maintained by the fact that we were communicating in highly controlled environments (i.e. the computer and phone). We could both be the versions of ourselves that the other hoped we were and I could even ignore the fact that he was an actor.

During the very beginning of our obsessive communiqué, I told him my circumstances—essentially, that I'd moved to New York from LA three months earlier and was returning to LA in a few weeks to pack up the remainder of my belongings, get rid of my car and head back for good. His response: "I live in LA but am from New York and have been wanting to move back forever." It was on!

Did I mention that he had two months of sobriety and had been heavily addicted to heroin? I don't think I did and that's perhaps because it wasn't something I chose to mention to myself, really, during this whirlwind romance. And look; I knew about dating newcomers. In fact, I'd judged many people for doing it!

There are all sorts of aphorisms floating around about why dating newcomers was a bad idea: "It's like networking in the nuthouse." "The odds are good but the goods are odd." I'd heard them all. And so I fell back on one of my favorite delusions: It'll be different for me. And that's how it happened that when I landed in LA a few weeks later for that aforementioned trip, he was at the airport to pick me up holding chocolates and a sign that read "Mrs." followed by his last name. Our plan was for him to help me pack my belongings and then we'd fly back to New York together. But we weren't going to be alcoholic about it—he would not move in with me. No, to start this relationship off in a healthy way, he was going to instead stay at a hotel down the street for a month as he looked for his own apartment.

I think I also forgot to mention that he chain-smoked and I'd quit smoking six years earlier, transitioning into that hypocritical ex-smoker who held her nose and gave disapproving looks whenever she happened to pass people puffing away on cancer sticks. His smoking was admittedly harder to ignore than his troubled past during that two-week period we were in LA, especially because we spent the majority of that time holed up in his apartment. But I found a way.

When we flew to New York, I dozed on his shoulder and marveled over how my life had changed so quickly. Clearly, I realized, all I had to do was make a radical move like leave the place I'd called home for the previous decade for the universe to reward me with a gorgeous boyfriend.

So he settled into his hotel as I unpacked my belongings; he wasn't nearly as helpful unpacking in New York as he'd been packing in LA since coming over to my apartment meant not smoking without the hassle of having to take an elevator downstairs every few minutes. After a few days of our going to dinners and meetings and cafes, I realized that he wasn't all that helpful in conversation, either; the guy really did not, I learned, like to talk. A week or two after that, I discovered that he didn't like doing much of anything. He confessed after one dinner where he'd only grunted a few words that he wasn't really one for eating out and much preferred to have pizza delivered to his hotel room. So I started spending a lot of time in that hotel room, too, where we ate pizza and watched TV as I tried to convince myself that second-hand smoke really wasn't that bad. Also worth mentioning: He'd semi-lost interest in sex by then—a side effect, he said, of the medication he was taking.

Ah yes, the medication. What I didn't know until he was settled in New York was that he was on a bevy of meds—not just the SSRIs that many people I know (including myself) take but several others, including Klonopin. My stance on taking drugs like Klonopin and Xanax for sober people is that it's fine as long as it's absolutely necessary and you're being honest with your sponsor about it. He assured me that he was and also that his shrink—who, I learned, he had phone sessions with three times a week—strongly supported him taking it. I chose not to question if this Klonopin-taking meant he was really an active user and not a newcomer.

By this point, he'd left the Do Not Disturb sign on the hotel door for so long that the cleaning staff had learned to ignore the room's existence and so it had essentially become a large ashtray with a bed and pile of empty pizza boxes mixed in. I knew we were miserable together but New Year's Eve was right around the corner and it was freezing cold and I just didn't think ending things with a guy who'd sort of moved 3000 miles to be with me would be a good idea for either of us right then. Maybe, I thought, he'd cheer up and get more engaged in life once the weather improved?

It was on New Year's Eve, though, that I reached my breaking point, finally telling him, after a silent pizza dinner, that I didn't think we were compatible after all. He didn't disagree with me but said, and I quote, "Look, I think we should be unhappy together a little longer and break up later." I didn't think that was a great idea so the conversation was over by 11:30 pm. There didn't seem to be much of a point in staying until the ball dropped so I walked back to my apartment in the pouring rain while revelers all around me excitedly counted down and kissed at the stroke of midnight.

It took a little bit longer for the real uncoupling to occur; he did, in fact, sign a lease on an apartment and even start leaving it occasionally. But it wasn't long before he decided to go back to LA officially and sublet that place to a friend.

Now the old-time-y slogan about dating newcomers—"Behind every skirt is a slip"—suggests not only that men are going to be the ones 13th stepping but that the 13th-stepper's sobriety may not survive the transgression. This was not true in my case but, at a certain point in recovery, I stopped thinking of relapse as an option. Many of us, remembering how depressed using and drinking made us toward the end, skip right from "I should have a drink" to "I should just end it all." And while I wasn't suicidal over the dissolution of my MySpace romance, I was extremely sad. It wasn't about him, really; that kind of sadness never really is about the person. I was sad about the dissolution of the fantasy that I could fall for a beautiful stranger without having to go through any painful and stressful dating, courtship and intimacy development.

He and I stayed friendly and he actually called me a year or so later, saying he was in trouble and asking if I could take him to a meeting. He sweated all the way through it and I didn't get too many details about what had led up to this. My emotional ties to him had pretty much disintegrated, which is to say I was able to just worry about him the way I'd worry about any semi-hope-to-die addict I knew. I didn't hear from him for a while after that but I saw that he landed a lead role on a huge TV show so I reasoned that he hadn't fallen completely off the rails.

Then one day, when I was sitting in a coffee shop in LA writing, my phone rang and I saw it was him. Not knowing if he was calling to tell me he was finally sober or that he needed emotional support (somehow those seemed the only two possibilities), I answered.

"Oh great, you picked up!" he exclaimed, sounding as ecstatic to talk to me as he had back in our MySpace courtship. "Can you do me a favor?"

I was a bit frightened. "Um, maybe?" I said.

"Okay so my friend and I have been playing online poker but the game has shut us out so we need someone to sign in through another IP address."

"What?" I asked, as much confused by what he was asking as I was dumbfounded that he'd asked me. I hadn't spoken to him in over a year. Was he high? Had he become a gambling addict? "Why you'd call me?" I finally added.

"I was trying to think of people I thought might be in front of their computer," he responded, not sounding remotely apologetic or uncomfortable.

It wasn't exactly the kind of reason you hope to get when an ex calls you out of the blue but did he even really count as an ex? I didn't know the answer to that but I did know I couldn't help him. And let's just say I communicated that so effectively that I haven't heard from him since.

I also haven't dated another newcomer or judged anyone else for doing it. Who am I to say what works for other people? I can only learn what works—and doesn't work—for me. Alas, I seem to ignore warnings about why not to do things since I'm still often convinced that the standard rules don't apply to me. For better or worse, I'm someone who needs to touch the burning oven to know it'll hurt me, too.

As for MySpace—well, I don't even remember my password.

The Yellow Brick Road

When I was a few years sober, I ended up choreographing *The Wiz* for a free rehab that housed recently incarcerated men in downtown LA. How a Marin County girl ended up trekking to the hood twice a week to teach a group of ex-cons how to do a munchkin dance isn't nearly as interesting as the fact that it happened at all.

In short: I didn't have any sponsees and was looking for a way to be of service. I toured the rehab and saw a sign that there were auditions for *The Wiz*.

"A musical!" I exclaimed to the person giving me the tour. "I love musicals!" I talked about how I'd had lead dancing parts in *Bye Bye Birdie*, *Hair* and *West Side Story* in high school and how I'd later danced and choreographed professionally. Before I knew it, I'd made the commitment.

To say I did not know what I was getting into would be the understatement of the decade. I seem to have this blind faith that can be considered wonderful or dangerous depending on the day but I just kind of naively assume if something's come along, it's meant to come along and I will be protected.

The faith was really, really blind in this case.

The fact is I was a woman showing up to teach a bunch of questionably sober ex-cons how to dance for a musical they were being forced to perform in if they wanted their parole officers off their respective backs.

In other words, they were not remotely interested in learning the munchkin dance I'd painstakingly choreographed in my living room.

A typical rehearsal found me teaching the dance and them sort of not really trying to learn it. Then they would ask me out. Or hand me love letters. Or give me gifts that they'd clearly stolen, usually clothing that was a few sizes too small.

I don't tell you this to be self-aggrandizing. I tell you this to explain that I was the only woman they'd been around in a long time and they didn't seem to understand why I'd want to show up twice a week for months at a time to teach a munchkin dance.

To be honest, I was starting to wonder the same thing.

But it was service! Service, as people in recovery often said, wasn't supposed to feel good! It was supposed to get you out of your head!

Get me out of my head this did, particularly when I would show up and see two guys nursing black eyes and be informed that they'd gotten in a fist fight over me. While I normally will accept any opportunity to get that damn ego of mine fed, I was starting to get freaked out.

But I kept at it, even though I would be faced with a new bunch of munchkins every week since most every resident either relapsed or was kicked out at some point. By the week of the show, there was actually only one guy who'd been a part of the group when we'd started a few months earlier and he wasn't, to be kind, Fred Astaire.

After all those months of driving there, pretending I wasn't a sheltered girl and that teaching ex-cons a munchkin dance was an appropriate use of my time, it was determined that none of the munchkins knew the dance. It was determined that I would have to be in the play, playing a munchkin, so the rest could follow my steps.

The show had to go on and go on it did. I'll tell you the truth: I killed as a munchkin. I know this because two of my friends came to see the show but I only learned it later since they both left at intermission—scared that they would be mugged or their cars would be stolen. That was really the first time I understood quite how dangerous the neighborhood was.

Years later, I encountered criminals of a different sort. These criminals were cleaner, a bit more suave and a whole lot more awful. These criminals hired me to edit a recovery magazine.

Now I've worked for so many crazy people that when the lackey who'd hired me explained that I was going to be taking orders from someone in prison, I didn't even blink.

Instead I asked, "What's he in for?"

Embezzlement, I was told.

I shrugged. At least, I figured, it wasn't murder.

The problem, as I saw it, wasn't that the guy running the show was a criminal. The problem was that he was an idiot. A few days into the gig, Lackey called to tell me that the celebrity we were planning to have on the cover was going to be replaced with a dog.

A dog?

"It's the boss," he said.

He explained that the boss really had a soft spot for this certain rehab that gave everyone a puppy.

We both laughed. Jesus.

Then Lackey said that maybe it would be better if I communicated with the boss directly.

And thus began a month of me learning how to communicate with prisoners. Yes, plural. Because, as it turned out, the boss wasn't the only person I was taking orders from. There was also a man we can call Gary. It was never clear to me who Gary was in relation to the boss—a lover, a prison mate, the guy he'd embezzled with? It clearly didn't matter. I grew accustomed to getting two prison-sent missives a day, always filled with terrible ideas that I always acted like I thought were great.

One day, one of these messages from Gary explained that he'd written a book and wanted me to write the foreword to it. He attached it.

Unsurprisingly, said book was unintelligible.

But I needed this job, I told myself.

I wrote him back that of course I would write the foreword.

A therapist would call my agreeing to do this subscribing to a "scarcity mentality." I thought of it as just doing what I had to in order to remain employed.

A few days later, after thinking it through and talking to my sponsor, I came to the conclusion that I hadn't been hired to add my name to illiterate books written by the incarcerated. I wrote Gary that I was very sorry but I couldn't write the foreword.

I went back to finishing the current issue. I continued to work long days, forwarding stories and ideas to Lackey and his lackeys. But suddenly, they had all gone MIA.

Two days later, I woke up to an email from Lackey saying that he was "beside himself" because he had received the galley for the September issue. The email accused me of hiring writers who were plagiarists and then listed a series of inadvertently hilarious accusations about editing stories badly and promoting my podcast on other sites. It concluded, "It is obvious we need to hire a forensic researcher to determine the extent of plagiarism, recycling, and exposure to claims of copyright infringement." He asked for my resignation, saying that this, "together with a crafted message, mutual release and confidentiality/non-disparagement would obviously be in your best interests as well as ours, and we could all avoid a public discussion about your departure."

We were, to put it mildly, not in Kansas anymore.

Now I'll admit I cried when I got this. It doesn't matter how outrageous someone's accusation is; it doesn't matter how illiterate the email; it doesn't matter that you know it's written by a pathetic lackey answering to the demands of a prisoner's friend, who happens to be his boss.

It sucks to be told you suck.

I let myself cry for a day.

A few days later, I had forwarded the email to several people who are far more intelligent and litigious than I am, and all of them pointed out that these people had a hell of a lot to lose. It's illegal, of course, to run a company out of prison.

For several weeks I received emails from someone at the company asking me to sign an NDA. The more I refused, the harder he pushed. I just kept saying no—that they were free to tell anyone they wanted that I hired plagiarists. Then a friend pointed out that since they had everything to lose and I had nothing to lose, they probably would be willing to pay me to keep quiet. My responses to the business affairs guy began to hint at the fact that I would keep mum on the way they were doing business if they paid out my contract.

The guy in business affairs didn't bite. He did, however keep asking me to sign something.

One day he stopped emailing.

Shortly after that, I realized what a blessing this was. If I asked to be paid to keep quiet about their criminal activities, wouldn't I be as bad as them?

The day I let go of this debacle is the day I decided I would never again work for crazy and abusive people.

But a crazy thing happened when I made that decision. My little side hustle—a company actually called Light Hustle Publishing, where I help thought leaders write and publish their books—took the f off. Suddenly, out of nowhere, something I'd always considered an adjunct income started bringing in more than editing the prison magazine did—by a landslide.

And that's not the only thing that happened. I also ran into a munchkin.

Yep! A few months ago, I was sitting on a couch in the VIP room of a rock show—in other words, the last place on earth one would expect for this to happen—when a guy came up to me and told me he was 14 years sober and I was a large part of it.

"I was one of your munchkins," he said. With tears in his eyes, he told me how much the play had meant to him and what a large part of that I was.

"I still remember the dance," he said.

I myself do not. But this encounter reminded me yet again that you never know what's going to happen. I never thought when I was teaching a bunch of seemingly indifferent ex-cons a dance that I'd run into one who told me that changed his life. I also never thought I'd be called a plagiarist by a wanna-be writer in prison.

I guess it comes down to this: my former munchkin, the criminal running the recovery magazine and the rest of us are all on our own yellow brick roads, headed to our own emerald cities.

How we dance on them is up to us.

Part 3
WHAT IT'S LIKE NOW

I'm Addicted to the Internet – So What?

I'm writing this while 30,000 feet in the air on my way to a gorgeous island. And yet all I can think about is one thing:

This plane does not offer Wi-Fi.

Not for any good reason, either; I'm flying to Hawaii, where plenty of Wi-Fi-equipped planes do fly. They just, the flight attendant told me, haven't gotten around to making this particular plane Internet-accessible.

My jaw hung open far longer than I expected it to when she explained this to me. Shocked, I turned to the man in the seat next to me.

"Did you hear that?" I asked. "I mean, what are we supposed to *do*?"

He was very kind and agreed with me that this turn of events was indeed horrifying, even though he didn't seem to have a laptop with him. I began semi-frantically going through my carry-on: What did I even have with me? What would I do for the entire five-hour flight? And what if the airport didn't have Wi-Fi when we landed? And the hotel? My mind churned with ever more terrifying possibilities.

This is how I used to feel about cocaine—though it was, of course, not appropriate to turn to a stranger back then to discuss the terror I felt at the concept of not being able to get my fix (though there weren't many people around me once I got to this point, anyway).

In both cases, it didn't take me too long to get addicted. I remember when the Internet first started. I remember dial-up. And I remember being outraged by the slowness of dial-up, which only seems notable now because I had barely gotten used to Internet speed at all back then. Yes, my outrage preceded technological advancement. I wasn't a full-blown addict at that point, though. I was capable of not checking my email for hours if I didn't have access to it and I had plenty of other ways to comfort myself during awkward moments or times when I had to wait in line.

Of course, I know I'm not alone with this and that smart phones supposedly did this to us. But really, didn't I also do this to myself? I'm the one who keeps checking my email and Instagram, after all. I've been complicit in my behavioral addiction.

Social media got me in its grasp right away. Getting validation for photos and quips hit my endorphins in the best way I could imagine—so much so that I began essentially considering my iPhone a dopamine dispenser. When I felt lonely and should probably have been reaching out to a friend or at least examining why I felt that way, I instead got into the habit of trying to think of something clever to say and then immediately switching over to my @ responses on Twitter to see how a bunch of strangers responded. Did they think I was funny? Clever? Talented? Sometimes non-strangers—that is, friends—responded or retweeted or favorited me as well but if I'm going to be honest, the responses from strangers somehow meant just as much.

My relationship with Facebook is arguably even more dysfunctional. I used to be on a TV show that no one in my real life had ever even heard of but seemed to big with people who spent a lot of time online, and I used to just accept everyone who sent me a Facebook request, which means that I rather quickly hit the 5,000 friend limit. I was then inundated by chat requests from people I didn't know. I would also meet people I'd want to add as Facebook friends but I couldn't add because I'd hit my friend limit. And so I deleted all the people I didn't know. That's when I made a rather disturbing discovery: The people who didn't know me cared a lot more about what I posted than the people who did. Photos that had previously attracted up to 100 comments and likes suddenly only received a few; the quips I'd been convinced by the reactions I'd been getting were pretty cute even less.

But no matter; I could still find a way to make my relationship with Facebook dysfunctional.

I started using it in a manner many people, alas, seem to: as reading material as I pored through other people's posts in order to, as people in recovery say, "compare and despair." Everyone I knew, it seemed, had a book being made into a movie, a perfect husband and even more perfect child or the best friends in the world. Even though I understood that Facebook life wasn't entirely reflective of real life, I still allowed myself to either seethe with jealousy or, far more commonly, use what other people seemed to be achieving as an emotional sledgehammer to beat myself up.

I'm relieved to report that my compare-and-despair habit diminished exponentially once I realized that we all have issues and most of us wouldn't trade ours for anyone else's if we actually knew other people's real stories. Still, I really don't make an effort to try to make my relationship with the Internet healthy.

I don't even bother shaming myself if I eat a meal in front of the computer. Plenty of times, when I'm out with people, I spend a decent amount of time wondering when would be too soon to check my phone. I used to get up do a 20-minute meditation first thing every morning but a few years ago, I started making sure that 20 minutes started just after I checked my phone to "make sure there aren't any emergencies." And I feel incredibly proud of myself if I manage to leave the phone in the car when I go on a hike.

Just what the eventual impact of my Internet addiction is going to be, I have no idea. Even the experts have a tough time coming up with a consensus on this whole issue. There are, after all, many different Internet addiction tests out there. Here's what I know: This addiction sure feels a lot less shameful and dangerous than my coke addiction did. But also my already short attention span is growing ever shorter as a result of my behavior and true serenity comes from being in the moment and not from checking out.

People growing up today, of course, have it much worse. Brains don't finish developing until the mid-20s so kids who are handed iPads before they can speak and given phones in grammar school grow accustomed to checking out during their formative years. How alarming this really is hasn't been determined yet, but there are studies aplenty that link social media and Internet use to an array of different issues—among them eating disorders and low self-esteem. One study reported that one in five high school students are hyper-texters (meaning they text 120 times a day or more) and one in nine are hyper-networkers (meaning they spend three or more hours a day on Facebook or other social networking sites) and that hyper-texters are more likely to binge drink or do drugs. But is a parent really supposed to worry because there's "an apparent link" between a teen's relationship with a cell phone and her potential relationship with heroin?

Really, to me, the whole Internet addiction playing field is a bit of a mess. While there's a 12-step program out there for this, I've heard that when you can find a meeting, no one shows up. Sure, there are treatment centers attempting to corner the market on Internet/gaming addiction but does that mean treatment is necessary or even a good idea? As a compelling piece in *Scientific American* asked, "What's to be done with an agony you're not sure you should feel?" The writer added, "The agonies of an established illness like alcohol addiction are well known—the looming grief or helplessness, a steady sinking into a deep and widening chasm. But what about those who seem to have an unlisted addiction, like excessive gaming? Is that even a thing?"

Here's what I think: Maybe, just maybe, my Internet addiction is okay. Sure, unplugging for a day or a weekend is probably a good idea—one I may even be willing to explore soon. I have no doubt that my life would be more serene if I had a more manageable relationship with the Internet. But, for now anyway, I'm going to allow myself to indulge. In other words, if a bottom is coming, I haven't hit it yet. In this case, digging doesn't feel so bad.

Yes, I Believe in God... Except When I Don't

I avoided recovery for years, like many do, because of the God thing.

It's not that I didn't believe in God. I believed in the existence of some benign being that wanted the best for me. My thoughts on this weren't, however, developed. My religious education was negligible and had nothing to do with spirituality. I spent Sunday school classes writing my name in bubble letters in my notebooks rather than paying attention and High Holy Day services sneaking outside to hang out with friends while my nearly narcoleptic dad slept through the rabbi preaching about the Torah. God was never a religious idea to me, nor was it something I thought about often. I just accepted the idea of God and put it out of my head. Cars need gas. Eggs need to be cooked or you'll get salmonella. God exists.

So I didn't avoid recovery because I didn't believe in God; I avoided recovery because those who talked a lot about God were creepy.

People told me to go to meetings anyway and I did. And oh yes, the folks there were indeed creepy. They said Higher Power instead of God but they weren't fooling me. And so I bought a couple books about why AA was for religious freaks and went on with my weekly routine of alcohol, coke, cigarettes and Ambien.

Then I got to the point where I was willing to try anything—even something I knew would be creepy—to find another way.

Fuck it. I would talk about God if I had to.

By the time I got into recovery and realized that believing in (let alone talking about) God wasn't actually a requirement for 12-step or necessary in order to stay sober, I had the most profound spiritual experience of my life. It was pretty simple, really: For years, I couldn't stop doing coke or drinking. Then I came into recovery and started following the suggestions I heard in 12-step rooms and from my rehab counselor and sponsor. Shortly after that, for reasons I'll never be able to explain, the desire to do drugs and drink disappeared. It was gone, like my tonsils had been after I'd had a tonsillectomy in my 20s. But there had been no surgery; the part of my brain that was convinced it couldn't survive without chemicals somehow switched off. Now, I am a very logical person and since this didn't make any logical sense, all I could (and can) conclude is that it was (and please understand how difficult it is for a person who abhors earnestness to write the following two words together) a spiritual miracle.

From that moment on, I was a believer.

I became one of those people who didn't even replace the word "God" with "Higher Power" in order to not alienate those in meetings who had an aversion to the G-word. I wasn't even embarrassed to share that my concept of God was pretty much the bearded dude in the sky. I'd hear other people talk about how sexist and ridiculous that was; I'd even heard some (okay, one girl) recite the Serenity Prayer with the word Goddess instead of God. I listened to all sorts of people talk about how they used doorknobs or the fellowship ("Group of Drunks") or their dog (God spelled backwards) as their Higher Power. I have a sponsee who used Cher. But mine was the guy in the sky and no one argued with it, the same way no one argued with the idea of Cher. God of your understanding it was.

I realize that, to some people, believing in God makes me sound like a simpleton and that there are many who think there's no way that the sort of tragedies that occur could possibly happen if there was any sort of higher being out there. I don't have justifications or explanations for what I think; I can't answer any specific questions about it and ultimately I see it as a choice; if it makes me feel better when I choose to believe in God, what's the harm? It's the way I think about horoscopes or vitamins or anything else that divides people into devotees and cynics: if you believe it, it becomes true for you.

For a while, this spiritual connection really worked. I felt safe and protected, consistently convinced that everything was unfolding exactly the way it was meant to. At about six months of sobriety, I lost my job—my dream job. I decided this was meant to happen, never spent a second sad about it, and within months had a much better situation worked out. I felt grateful for what I had and unconcerned with what I didn't. Then that gratitude only seemed to beget more and more to feel grateful for. The program worked! Recovery was wonderful! I related to those ridiculous people who claimed that they were grateful to be alcoholics!

And then....

Screech.

It changed.

Oh boy, did it change. And then, eventually, mercifully, it changed back. You could say my recovery has basically been a vacillation between those two states. When I get into the place where I'm not connected, when I can't seem to have any sense of spirituality no matter how much I meditate or how hard I pray, when I feel like I haven't gotten anything I deserve and never will, I can barely remember what that grateful, protected place feels like. And then when I veer back into gratitude and a spiritual connection, it seems impossible to believe I won't be able to stay there.

The challenge is trusting that the next wave of belief will come when I'm not feeling it. It's knowing that even if praying and writing and meditating and talking to my sponsor and sharing about wanting to feel some spiritual connection isn't working the way cocaine used to—with that inhalation up the nose and instant mood change—that's only because it just hasn't happened yet. All I have to do is be patient and not make up stories about how I'm never going to feel better. But here's the ironic or unfair or just plain fucked up part: in the beginning of my sobriety, this was easy because I'd just experienced the miracle of having my desire to use removed. Every day that passes, I move further away from that and therefore have to work harder to feel it.

Over the years, my concept of God has changed. I don't really envision a guy with what is now considered a hipster beard chilling on some clouds but I don't picture a doorknob or a dog or Cher either. I think of it now more as being aligned with an energy out there or the universe as a whole. I imagine, as time passes, it will continue to change. And who knows? Maybe I'll get another miracle.

Becoming the Person I Drank to Be

When I was 12 years old, my family went on a cruise where I met and became fast friends with a 13-year-old girl. Let's call her Jane.

Jane was effortlessly cool. She drew in both kids and adults. And when I heard my mom call her fearless, I decided I wanted to be fearless, too.

I wouldn't say I was especially fearful before that. But I was a little on the shy side, and I hated being described that way. It was the word people always used when talking about my dad and I wanted to be more like my mom.

I decided that I would be fearless, too.

Without knowing it, Jane was my teacher for the two weeks on that cruise. We ran around that boat playing ping pong, going to the movie screenings and even dating two brothers (12-year-old dating, which is to say we called it dating but all we did was talk about how we liked them and they liked us and play ping pong against them).

By the time the boat pulled up to shore, I had made my transition.

Except that it wasn't a complete 180. While I believe I am a natural extrovert and part of what happened on that trip was me coming into myself, I still had many moments of extreme shyness and insecurity—times when I felt nearly paralyzed by social anxiety. I learned to push through those times. I would curl my toes in my shoes until it passed. While it didn't happen a lot, it happened.

And then I discovered drinking.

I will never forget the magical night when I discovered that alcohol could make me into the fearless person I'd always wanted to be. I was a freshman in high school and my friends and I were at a party at a senior's house. As I drank a beer, the guy who was the dictionary definition of Big Man on Campus—a guy I considered far more Greek God than high school senior—walked in. Let's call him Matt.

Everyone was in love with Matt. When Matt played soccer, the entire female school body would sit on the sidelines and sigh that his legs were like works of art. It was a widely established fact that being around Matt meant losing the ability to speak.

But when Matt walked by me a few minutes later, I followed him to where he was waiting in line for the bathroom.

"I have Matt + Anna written on my binder," I announced by way of introduction. I didn't think about the potential repercussions of making this (entirely true of course) confession could be or what he might say. The words were just there.

He smiled. "That's funny," he responded. "I have it written on my binder, too."

And that's when I knew it: Alcohol not only made me who I wanted to be but also got me everything I wanted.

(To be clear, I never really "got" Matt—he had an equally perfect senior girlfriend—but that night was the beginning of an outrageously flirtatious friendship. Unfortunately, I could only participate in it at parties; when he tried to talk to me at school, in the clear sober light of day, I could only utter monosyllabically in his presence.)

I moved on, of course, from Matt. While my other high school relationships with boys were not that dramatic, from that point forward, they always involved drinking. When I was drinking, I could be Jane—the girl who was fearless without having had to decide to be that way.

The longer I'm sober, the more I see that the way alcohol removed my social fears is what I liked the most about it. I could be the cool girl without effort, without having to worry about what I said, without picking at my cuticles to alleviate my anxiety. I was only semi-conscious of this particular attribute of drinking, though I do remember thinking, if I ever met a guy I liked during the day, that I wished I could meet him at night. My nighttime self, I told myself, was much better than my daytime one.

I honestly didn't think of it as my drunk self and sober self. My "nighttime self" sounded much better in my mind.

As anyone who gets sober after having spent most of his or her life drinking can attest, the original process is terrifying. I didn't admit to myself I was scared because I told myself I wasn't scared, let alone terrified, of anything. I'd driven to the hood to buy coke from Mexican gangsters. I'd snorted heroin and allowed a photographer in Paris to take nude photographs of me. Scared? Please.

Without realizing it, I'd internalized the idea that I was not allowed to feel fear so instead it came up as other things: either social anxiety or anger and sadness. At the beginning of sobriety, it was all anger and sadness. When that passed—when I actually began to be grateful—the fear morphed into social anxiety. I started going to meetings but I'd arrive late and leave early so I didn't have to deal with how scared I was of all the people there.

Then, after a slip when I was roughly six-and-a-half months sober, my sponsor suggested that I get truly invested in the program and start making friends in the rooms. I resented that. I told her I wasn't scared and reminded her that she was my friend. All she said was, "I'm your sponsor."

The next day at a meeting, fighting every instinct in me, I turned to a girl sitting next to me and introduced myself. She was friendly, not intimidating at all, and she ended up inviting me out with her friends for that night. I quickly fell in with her group and suddenly, I was more than dipping my toe in social sobriety; I was going out all the time and in many ways more social than I'd ever been. In most ways, this was glorious; I'd spent the previous few years holed up in my apartment with only cats and cocaine for company. But in retrospect there were many nights when I was fighting fear and insecurity. Feelings were still very new to me and cigarettes and Red Bull could only do so much to shroud them.

I can safely say now that the social fear is almost entirely gone and I can't even begin to list the fears I've conquered, from rappelling down buildings to going on live TV to speaking in front of auditoriums to publishing books. I'm not sure when the terror disintegrated but everything I know how to do I learned in recovery. Through that, the personality I craved as a kid has revealed itself to be a part of me.

Here's hoping Jane would be proud.

I'm the Weirdest Codependent in the World

Over the past few weeks, I've listened to a trainer pontificate on adoption, a tarot card reader lecture about treating bacterial infections and a gynecologist go off about brain scans. In all three cases, I took what the person was saying as utter gospel. They each spoke with tremendous self-confidence and so I immediately assumed that what I knew about these topics was utterly wrong and that the person doing all the talking was the reigning expert on the matter.

All three times, I didn't even realize I was buying everything these people were saying as the inarguable truth until I spoke to someone else; in every case, the second person I talked to pointed out how many people spout off on things they don't know about—something I of course already know but had completely forgotten in the face of these strident conversations. Once talking to the second round of people, all anxiety those initial chats had sparked dissipated entirely.

All three times, I couldn't hold onto what I knew to be true until someone else confirmed it.

When I was talking to another friend about this—one of those typical conversations people in recovery have where you diagnose and often pathologize things about yourself that a non-sober person either wouldn't have a label for or even notice—I mentioned how codependent I was. She looked shocked and told me I was the least codependent person she knew.

I argued with her, explaining that I did all sorts of things where I put other people's opinions and needs before mine and where I people-pleased in order to avoid someone potentially having an issue with something I did. She wasn't convinced and said that she'd almost never seen someone who was so... I'll confess that she started to say the word "confrontational" but then stopped and described it as "unafraid to tell people" how I felt. (Jury still out on whether the word substitution had to do with her own codependence.)

What she said had never really occurred to me. So, like anyone endlessly fascinated by herself who revels in being the "most" anything, even when the thing isn't positive, I diagnosed myself again: I'm the weirdest codependent in the world.

The best way I can break it down is that I don't worry at all about saying something that could be perceived as harsh if I'm a) annoyed or b) feel like it's absolutely necessary in the situation (these are connected; when I'm annoyed, changing the circumstances feels necessary). A comes up more frequently than B, simply because I annoy easily (whistling, singing, talking loud, gum chewing, smoking—all of these and more are on my intolerance list). In those situations, I will, in a way that is almost always incredibly inappropriate, have no hesitation when asking the person to stop or just glare until they do. (As a pack-a-day smoker for 13 years who's been—forgive me—smober for the past 17, I'm as hypocritical as can be.) In my office, where many businesses share the same space, I once approached someone who had consistently loud phone conversations with a hostile, "You realize we can all hear everything you're saying" before I ever introduced myself. (We ended up becoming friends because, well, he's more tolerant than I am; he also has much quieter phone conversations now.)

When it comes to giving writers notes on stories of theirs that I'm editing, I get right down to it without hesitating. I have absolutely no fear about any potential confrontation in those situations. Likewise, in 12-step meetings, I'll share whatever I feel like I need to get out without considering the fact that people might have a problem with or judge it.

But then I veer into massive people pleasing. You should hear how much I apologize when I think I might be annoying someone. I actually almost always end up annoying myself in these cases but the need to do this often feels like a compulsion.

More codependence: When I used to write profiles on celebrities and other people for magazines, I always had trepidation when it came to writing anything remotely negative. What if the person sent me an angry email or, even worse, I ran into them and had to handle an in-person negative reaction? I have a friend, a far more successful journalist than I ever was, who writes about the most powerful and well-known people in the world and has no trouble laying out her strongest opinions on them, even when those opinions would surely cause the subject somewhere between serious agita and serious rage. She's one of the nicest people I know so it's not some misguided hostility, just an honest assessment of who the person she's writing about is. I've asked her how she can handle knowing that these supremely powerful people will surely resent her and what's more that she could run into them, and she just shrugs, not understanding that I couldn't write the way she does even if the person inarguably deserved it.

But then, when it comes to writing about myself, I'll commit to paper (and magazine page and Internet) some of the least appealing revelations imaginable without even considering what people might think. I somehow feel it is absolutely my right and almost duty to be a chronic confessionalist and compulsively honest in my writing. I'm even fine with the character-assassinating comments that can come along with this writing habit.

Oh, but then we swing back into codependence land. Have I ever been able to tell a guy I've started dating that I'm not interested in him? Er, not really. My go-to is that I'm "not available right now." I literally cannot get the words "I'm just not interested in you" out of my mouth. The conclusion I tend to draw about this is that it's hurt when men have told me they're not interested in me and I don't want to cause someone to feel the way I've felt. But am I that kind? This doesn't feel like it necessarily comes from an altruistic place. All I know is that I've said, "It's not you—it's me" more times than I can count.

And don't even get me started on the topic of bringing a friend who won't know anyone at a party as my plus one. Ack, the anxiety and pressure I feel to make sure they're okay! Every time I have a birthday dinner, gathering all the disparate friends together for a situation where I'm the only thing they may have in common, I'm in a codependent panic almost the entire time. Is my coworker finding enough to talk about with my high school friend? Are the sober people talking character defects and God and freaking everyone else out? None of this stops me from having these, of course;

as one more example of me pathologizing myself, I'm an occasional masochist.

Oh, and then there are those situations where I can tell someone isn't comfortable around me; in my efforts to put these people at ease, I'll make myself more uncomfortable then they ever were. On that note, those people who can have long periods of silence while with other people? I'll sit there mystified by them as my brain all but shrieks, "Silence must be filled!"

So where does this leave me? I'm not really sure. I didn't relate at all when I checked out CODA meetings, didn't really feel a connection to the bible for codependents, *Codependent No More*. I can surely focus more on seeing "out rather than in," as my therapist calls it, or I can just accept that there are times I place other people's needs way ahead of mine, even if I'm imagining their needs, and other times when I don't. And I can continue to take pride in calling myself the weirdest codependent in the world.

What Happens to an Irritable Person on a Meditation Retreat?

Until a few years ago, the words "meditation" and "retreat" did not go together in my world, in any capacity. Truthfully, the word "retreat" never entered my vocabulary much at all, unless it somehow involved a spa treatment. But suddenly it seemed as if people were retreating. People were becoming retreat-ers.

It was time for me to join the fray.

Especially because the retreat I'd decided to sign up for was being led by Thom Knoles, the man who'd taught me meditation nearly a decade ago. The form of meditation he teaches, Vedic meditation, is a derivative of the Transcendental Meditation technique taught by Maharishi Mahesh Yogi, and I've been practicing it for roughly 20 minutes every morning and 20 minutes every afternoon most days since I learned 15 years ago.

Still, meditation, for me, has always been a solitary act: Something I do, in a cool, quiet room—preferably my bedroom—with the windows closed. During Thom's visits to Los Angeles over the years, I've occasionally joined in the group meditations he's led, where I've encountered hordes of people who have told me how much they love meditating in a group setting. I've nodded and then contemplated murder as I tried meditating next to them but found myself horribly distracted by their coughing or rustling around or loud breathing.

There were benefits of meditation that these coughers and breathers spoke of that I felt I wasn't necessarily getting. They talked about things like "feeling at one with the world" and "entering new states of consciousness" and "developing a magnanimous feeling" toward their fellow man. I got the feeling that if I breathed too heavily next to them while meditating—and for all I knew, I did—they found it not irritating but actually somehow beautiful.

It was time to take my practice deeper. It was time to acknowledge, first, that what I had was a practice. I realized that the role I'd given meditation in my life was that of "efficiency generator": I always felt energized after one of my 20-minute sessions, especially after the afternoon one, because it usually provided me with enough energy to write for another few hours. But I wanted more.

The retreat I signed up for was in the Catskills town of Phoenicia, at Menla Mountain Retreat, a 320-acre property operated by the US Tibet House. After spending a few days in Manhattan, I took a Trailways bus out to Phoenicia, passing Woodstock and enough Catskills towns to feel like I'd somehow accidentally landed in *Dirty Dancing*.

Once I arrived at Menla, I met the other members of the group: Primarily 30- and 40-something creative professionals, along with a smattering of 50-somethings and two 20-something brothers whose father had recently gone on one of Thom's retreats. Many of us were experienced meditators—some had even been on other retreats with Thom before—but there were newcomers as well.

We were there to learn what's known as "rounding." When I'd first heard this word, I'd pictured each of us bent over in half, arms hanging to the side, moving around in circles—some sort of a leftover image I must have had in my head from watching a group of Deadheads at a show I'd been dragged to in high school. But rounding was actually, I soon learned, a series of asanas (or yoga poses) and Pranayam (or breathing techniques) that we were instructed to do before beginning one of our 20-minute meditations.

The poses were quite basic—what Power Yoga enthusiasts in LA or New York would surely sniff at—and apparently it was their very basic-ness that was so important. We were told not to make any serious effort at them: If we bent over and, say, our arms didn't touch the ground, we weren't supposed to stretch until we reached the floor, the way we're encouraged to do in most fitness classes, but to dangle where we were. The Pranayam consisted of plugging one nostril and breathing in, then switching to plug the other nostril and breathing out—for five minutes. Doing all of that—the asanas followed by the Pranayam followed by one of our regular 20-minute meditation sessions—was doing a round. And what were we supposed to do after completing a round? Why, more rounding!

While this sounds like it would be tedious, for some reason I found it anything but. Of course, what I had motivating me was the promise that, after rounding retreats, stress that had accumulated for years would literally drop away.

Many retreaters stayed in the main lecture hall and did their rounds together—each taking their own spot, marked by a yoga mat, against the wall—while others went off to round in their rooms or even outside. I started in the main room but, despite the stress falling away from me, I was still me—which means that when one of my fellow retreaters rounded off his round by falling asleep and snoring, I found myself wanting to roll up my yoga mat and toss it in his direction. Off to my room I went.

Rounding was broken up by meals—all terribly healthy, except for one lunch that inexplicably included chocolate chip cookies—and lectures by Thom, about everything from the long-term benefits of meditating ("Over time, it makes you sort of mentally deficient at getting stressed—in the same way that if you dip a cloth into dye, eventually the color will start to stick") to understanding our relationship to joy ("Object Referral Happiness means that the object world has arranged itself into a set of circumstances that fit our idea of happiness whereas Self-Referral Happiness comes from stepping beyond thought into the field of being, where we can say, 'If my whole world is taken away, that's okay because I'll just create a whole new world'"). During the first few lectures, I noticed a lot of people placing their phones on the stage next to Thom. I was so relaxed that my brain apparently wasn't working clearly and I assumed they were doing that because they didn't trust themselves not to be distracted by Twitter or Words with Friends or Facebook while he was talking. It was only during the last lecture that I realized they were all recording his words.

The stress relief that would come from two straight days of rounding would, Thom promised, be noticeable: the retreat ended on a Monday morning and he swore that by Wednesday, we'd feel, undeniably, a previously not-experienced level of joy. And call it the power of suggestion or just call it a process that works but by that Wednesday, I was back in LA and I was, indeed, delighting in my life. The feeling lasted—well, a few days at least. But a few days of pure delight for someone who finds herself regularly wanting to smack a fellow meditator who's coughing may be some sort of a record. If I want to get it back—well, that's what another retreat is for.

My Addiction Was a Family Disease

My parents started off pretty relaxed about drugs—by which I mean that they were open with me that they had smoked pot and they didn't subscribe to any alarmist tactics when it came to warning me about any drugs. Whether this was ultimately good or bad, I have no idea. But it seemed like the right way: We lived in Marin County and this was the '80s, which meant that members of the Grateful Dead frequented the same local supermarket as us. Being alarmist about drugs in the '80s was not the Marin way.

Still, my older brother didn't give my parents any preparation for me. He was a straight arrow, a computer and video game kid before such a persona was a known cultural entity. I was not. And, as my teenage years progressed, I started to get in trouble—for shoplifting, for having alcohol on me while riding in my friend's car, for throwing massive, cop-raided parties while my parents were out of town. None of this was par for the course for my Harvard-educated dad, PhD-earning mom and D&D-loving brother. It's safe to say that my parents were thrown for a bit of a loop.

When I say my parents, I really mean my mom, because my dad wasn't at all involved in any day-to-day parenting. Compared to other mothers and daughters I knew as an adolescent, my mom and I had a really good relationship—which is to say that I didn't slam doors and tell her to fuck off, and we actually had honest discussions about some things. But when I started to get in trouble, a lot of that changed.

Looking back, it's clear that my mom didn't know what to do and that my behavior scared her. I can't say I wouldn't have reacted the same way in her position. But it just so happened that her reaction was exactly what I did not need. After I was busted for shoplifting and later for alcohol possession, I felt ashamed and not a lot else. I didn't understand—or even try to understand—why I was doing these things. I didn't have the vocabulary or awareness to articulate that I felt so uncomfortable that I needed to do things that helped me to escape myself, that I had no ability to just be in the moment and that I was too terrified to even admit to myself or anyone else that I was scared.

My mom didn't yell and scream; that was never her way. Instead she shut down. She spoke to me about what I'd done in a voice so cool that I felt like I could have skated over it. To me, this was far worse than hearing anger or disappointment; I felt, when she talked like that, as if my behavior had been so bad that she'd actually stopped loving me. My shame intensified.

There were more incidents. When I was 16, Mom happened upon a passage in my diary where I wrote about smoking pot and rubbing cocaine on my lips to experience what I called "Numb-y Gum-y." That same year, she came across some nitrous oxide capsules that I used to do whip-its. Her responses to these things were also icy. More shame followed.

There were a number of issues going on in my family at the time—issues that unarguably harmed me and made me feel unsafe at home. But I think what was even worse than feeling unsafe was the feeling that I was a fuck-up. I felt like there was something terribly wrong with me. Like I was different than they were. Like I was wrong—not just that I was doing things that were wrong but that my very existence in itself was wrong.

It is my belief—though I should mention that my family does not agree with me about this—that "Anna is the problem child" became something of a family meme. I'd had colic as a baby, and always heard stories about how much I'd screamed and cried and how no one had been able to stand it. The point of these stories, it seemed to me, wasn't how sad it was that I'd been so inconsolable as a baby but that my being so troubled had driven everyone else crazy.

And my troubles continued. I'd apparently had bad temper tantrums as a child. Then, as a teen, I had chronic headaches and insomnia. The fact that I had a headache when I was 16—and when I say a headache, I mean that for one year straight, my head ached around the clock—was dealt with the way things were dealt with back then: I went to the best neurologist my parents could find. He plugged me into a biofeedback machine meant to measure my stress level, gleaned that I was a 10 on a scale of 1-10 and prescribed me painkillers. I still remember my confusion over the euphoria I felt when I took them; no one had told me it was going to get me high and so, I reasoned, my elation was due to the absence of pain. Of course, daily opioid use meant building up a tolerance fairly quickly, so I went from the first prescription to an even stronger opioid, and when that stopped working, I graduated to an even stronger one. Like I said, different times. Eventually, thankfully, the headaches dissipated—but my chronic pain just made me feel even more like something was wrong with me.

So you could say that the addictions I picked up as a result of both these circumstances and my genetic predisposition—I believe that my now-deceased maternal grandmother and grandfather were both addicts—made sense. I am not making excuses. I was—and still am, at times—selfish, narcissistic, attention-seeking and all sorts of other things that are no one's fault but my own. I'm not trying to point fingers. Plenty of kids grew up in far more damaging environments with far more of a genetic predisposition and never became addicted to anything. And my parents did many of the so-called right things; my mom helped me to find the best therapist I could. And I tried to share with him all that was going on, and even succeeded at times.

But I do think things might have turned out differently if my problems had been dealt with as family issues, rather than "Anna issues." It would have been better if we'd discussed and dealt with some of the dysfunction we lived in that exacerbated my genetic predisposition, and if I hadn't been left feeling like I alone was the problem. It would have been better, in other words, if I hadn't been the identified patient.

Back then, people didn't throw around terms like "blaming the addict" or "identified patient." Today we do—and we know that having a family surround an addict in a loving, supportive way is crucial.

And because parents today are lucky enough to have information like this available to them in a way that my generation's parents did not, I'd encourage them to approach this issue with all the awareness possible, as well as the love. But it's not just on them; addicted children often spend a lot of time blaming their parents for every little thing they did wrong—something I know only too well because, for a long time, I was leading the charge. The way I see it now, finger-pointing is not only a waste of time but also a distraction from the real problem.

The other thing I've realized: if you're a teenager who keeps a diary, for God's sake put a lock on it.

Congrats on Quitting Sugar, Now Let Me Act Out On My Addiction in Peace

I do not have sugar sobriety.

I didn't, in fact, realize that people talked about giving up sugar in this way until I got sober. Yes, I've been all too aware of the fact that sugar is addictive. I've read the stories; I've seen the facts. I knew about the food programs. I still didn't know that this was a thing people counted days on and talked about like it's as dangerous as juggling with knives.

I, like many of my generation, watched Saturday morning cartoons with bowls of Frosted Flakes, Lucky Charms and Corn Pops in my lap, shoveling the delicious, sugary bits of heaven doused in milk into my mouth, thinking that I was having a perfectly healthy breakfast. (I didn't, of course, think that way then; this was during the era when I graded my days in my journal and any day where I got to go to McDonald's got an automatic A+.) Still, I certainly didn't know I was nurturing an addiction.

But then tragedy struck the David abode. I innocently went away to camp when I was eight and came home to learn that my parents had read a horrible, dangerous book during my absence— something written by a sadist named Pritikin. These parents of mine lapped up everything this evil man put out there and my brother and I were hapless victims. Gone were the Milano cookies and M&M's that had once filled our cupboard. Our snack cupboard, in fact, was mostly bare, save some carob chips that even in my most desperate state I couldn't bring myself to snack on. Meat had pretty much been excised as well, but that's a separate topic altogether. I remember whole wheat pasta being the tastiest dinner option— mostly, I recall, we survived on meals that tasted like cooked twigs; I'm still not sure what those foods originally were.

I tried to talk sense into my parents—to no avail. They were used to my nagging (my first sentence, if family lore can be trusted— and though it often cannot, I believe this one—was, "It's not fair"). By this point, they were immune to my complaints. I remember going on walks around the neighborhood with my mom in the evenings, smelling BBQs and doing my best to convince my mom that she and my dad had clearly lost it. She was always bemused, never remotely willing to succumb to my guilt trips.

While the David Pritikin phase turned out to be blessedly ephemeral, it feels like it lasted several decades. And since, like many people, I was once on a never-ending quest to blame my parents for everything, I justified the terrible food I ingested as an adult as a rebellion against that Pritikin period during my formative years. In college, I returned, in fact, to Lucky Charms and Corn Pops as a reasonable breakfast.

And so my predilection for sugar continued.

When you quit drinking, people (gentle, wise people) will often tell you that because alcohol has so much sugar in it, it's okay for you to continue to consume it without feeling guilty. It's even in the program literature! Though I was far more of a cocaine user and pill taker than I was a drinker, I latched onto this justification with relish (or actually candy). When I quit smoking roughly nine months after getting sober, I had even more justification; where else would I get my oral fixation satisfied?

And so my predilection for sugar continued.

But this other thing happens when you've been sober a while, particularly if you live in LA. The people around you start a) believing they're addicted to everything (*My Strange Addiction* didn't help this) and b) improving their lives in as many external ways as possible. I can't claim to not be on this train myself; in addition to quitting smoking, I upped the exercise to a potentially addictive degree and have at times have even broken my nasty caffeine addiction.

Yet I steadfastly cling to the sugar, despite the fact that I know I'm addicted, if only because I once had to leave a friend's dinner party because she didn't bring out the dessert soon enough. At least part of my reticence has to do with fear around the detox. I've seen people quit it and go into deep depressions. Who needs that? Isn't life already hard? Haven't we given up enough?

Apparently not. And those who are sober from sugar never tire of telling you as much. Oh, and rest assured they're not talking just about cookies and cake; they will gossip about people who claim to be sober from sugar but actually eat fruit. Which leads to my main question here: Why are people who are off sugar so self-righteous?

I've had people lecture me at length about how I'm killing myself with my continual use of this white powder. These people often go on tirades about flour as well, but it's the sugar thing that really gets them going. I've listened to a shrink I had on my podcast call those who eat sugar in moderation "non-practicing bulimics." I've felt trapped in shame-inducing sugar quitting conversations where I've been able to do nothing but nod and brainstorm ways to get away. I've watched people's faces get red and heard their voices rise as they railed against addicts of my kind.

The most interesting aspect of this, to me, is that these have pretty much all been sober people. This is to say that these have all been people who I know are non-judgmental about the drinking and drugging habits of their fellows. One of the most common misconceptions non-sober people seem to have is that we sober folks are all sitting around with our mental dossiers compiling judgments about people who drink and thinking they need to put down all chemicals too. Yet most all sober people I know feel that those who can drink or do drugs responsibly by all means should. Even in the face of a clear alcoholic, most do their best to not ever let the person feel judged because they know that this would be the last thing that would motivate them to change.

So why, then, is the attitude the opposite for those self-righteous sugar sober people? My friend once (half) joked that "sugar sober" people are like this because they don't have that soothing white powder to temper their rage. This was before she casually (and semi-infuriatingly) gave up sugar herself. Despite the fact that she was an enthusiastic sugar addict and seemed to have no trouble making this transition, I'm happy to report that she doesn't lecture me at all about this, though this could be because she and I have regularly complained to each other about these folks.

So this is what I have to say to you people who are off sugar: I'm eating, as I type, a dark-chocolate-covered acai berry—that's right, a superfood! It is delicious. And look, if it turns out that this is leading me down the devil's path, I'll discover that in my time.

Facing Fear Sober

The reason I got sober isn't that I thought sobriety sounded like a great idea. It was actually something I thought that only a complete loser would embrace. It was the act, I was certain, of a person with absolutely no other options.

The problem was that I was that person with no other options. And I was so depressed by my cocaine-cigarette-vodka-Ambien diet—and the cycle of trying to quit it and not being able to—that I figured anything, even sobriety, had to be better.

So one morning I called my mom and told her that I was a coke addict and that I was in serious trouble. I don't know what was different about that morning. Maybe nothing was different but I just had a moment where I wasn't able to talk myself into continuing on the path I was on.

Now, my mom is one of those mothers who would love to get both of her children back into her womb, if possible. But barring that, she'll settle for living back in the house we grew up in. Barring that, she'll take living in Northern California. I was living in LA. So that morning I called her, she said, "LA's been terrible for you. Go get in your car and drive home."

I drove there, completely despondent. If there was anything that sounded more depressing than being sober in LA, it was being sober in my hometown. But like I said, I didn't have any options. I ended up talking to my parents and my step-dad and a therapist about what I'd been doing—telling them the whole story and not just the edited version I'd been giving them for years. I admitted that I spent entire weeks doing cocaine alone, that I didn't have any friends anymore, that I sometimes took so much Ambien after getting wired that I worried one morning I just wouldn't wake up. They were rightfully alarmed and agreed to help pay for rehab. Somehow I talked them into helping to pay for a rehab in LA and not in Northern California. And somehow I talked that rehab, an inpatient program, into letting me do outpatient since I didn't want to have to quit the job I was barely hanging onto.

But this rehab, and sobriety, turned out to be nothing like I expected. The people there weren't shuffling around in grey sweaters, lamenting their lives. They were vibrant and hilarious and very much engaged in life in a way that none of the drug addicts I'd been around had been. And they were talking about things I not only related to but had long felt and never said out loud because I'd assumed no one would understand. They talked about their negative thinking—about how they'd wake up and think life was so dismal that they couldn't do anything but try to escape their thoughts through drugs. They talked about desperately trying to quit—about wanting to stop with everything in them—and not being able to, that decision to pick up again happening so quickly that they never even realized it was a decision. And they talked about ways of improving how they felt that had never occurred to me: about how trying to help other people gave them relief, about how it was their chronic self-obsession that kept them feeling so bad. They talked about how even though they thought obsessively about themselves, they also never felt like they were enough; I learned the expression that had summarized the previous three decades of my life: "I'm the piece of crap in the center of the universe."

If they'd been sober a while, they talked about finding happiness—and not through getting "cash and prizes," like the job or relationship they wanted, which is what I'd always called happiness. They talked instead about not needing to get the job or relationship they wanted in order to feel good. And my ears really perked up when they talked about resentments; I had a long list of people that had wronged me and I was always eager to extract vengeance somehow. But again they said surprising things: they talked about how it was in seeing the large part they'd played in their problems that they were able to forgive those other people. I did what they suggested and, really quickly, realized the strangest thing of all: I didn't want to drink anymore. I didn't even want to do cocaine. By just doing what these people suggested I do—which happened to radically alter my perception of every aspect of my life—it was like the part of me that craved alcohol and drugs, that had to leave town in order to escape the lure of cocaine and even then scrounged up coke wherever I was, had been removed. And it was a good thing, too, because I had essentially been sleepwalking through my life—walking and talking but emotionally and spiritually and intellectually frozen in time—so I had a lot of catching up to do. Finally I could actually figure out how to live.

The first element to learning how to live, I quickly learned, was facing my fears.

As far as I understand things now, I've struggled with three main fears my whole life—the fear that I'm stupid, the fear that I'm doing everything wrong and the fear that I'll lose everything I have and fail to get everything I want. But I didn't always know that.

When I first got sober, I was told by people who'd been sober longer that I lived with "a hundred forms of fear." I was told that fear ruled my every thought, feeling and action. I thought these people were a little dramatic; sure, I felt scared sometimes but not all that much. In many ways, I protested, I was fearless.

This was before I realized that I had a voice ruling everything I did and told me terrible things. I'm not crazy, I don't hear voices, I just heard one and its running commentary was a brutal combination of every negative thing anyone had ever said to me my whole life. It would tell me that I was stupid, that I was doing everything wrong, that everyone who mattered to me would leave me and that I didn't deserve what I had. It was only when I'd been sober at least five years that I even realized I was ruled by this voice—that I'd actually taken my fears and, too fearful to admit that I was scared, turned them against me. Rather than comforting myself through what scared me, I was taunting myself with these fears as if they were real and therefore not even giving myself a fighting chance.

So I started to think about the things I told myself and then present myself with this scenario: if I had a small, precious child I was caring for, would I tell her that she was an idiot and that no one would ever love her? Of course not! And if I wouldn't do that to a fictional child, why would I do it to myself? I began to write down the incredibly cruel things I told myself and learned to differentiate between what was a real thought and what was one of my fears turned against me. The process sucked; it took years to undo. But at a certain point, that horrible voice—the voice of my fears—

disappeared. It still comes back sometimes. Something will scare me—usually information that another person has something I think I should have—and the voice will turn on. But I've learned to recognize it and know it's not real. I've also learned that my fear can take all sorts of other forms. I rarely think the sentence, "I'm scared" because I internalized long ago that only weak people thought like that. So my psyche devised an entirely counterproductive system that makes fear register as all sorts of other feelings: tired, for example. Or nauseous. Indifferent. "I just don't feel like doing that" may, from me, mean "I'm scared to do that."

The fact that I now know this about myself, and can therefore move through it, has changed everything for me. I feel these days like I get to walk around with someone else's brain—the brain of someone who really, genuinely likes herself. And while I'm grateful to be rid of the obsessions I used to have to drink and do cocaine, I think I'm even happier to have shut the fear voice down.

But I Thought the Rules Didn't Apply to Me?

I can't believe this is happening but it is.

Yep, it's true. I'm growing older.

Look, I get it—most of us are appalled by aging. But I feel like it's different for me. Every day that it happens, which is to say every day, I feel more and more like one of those people you hear interviewed on NPR after they've survived a disaster—the ones who say, "I'd always heard about this happening to other people. I just never thought it would happen to *me*."

In other words, I'm flummoxed, stymied and every other SAT word we had to memorize over the fact that time is passing and with it, I am aging. Because I truly never, ever, ever thought it would happen to me.

I'm biologically programmed to be shocked by this turn of events. Both my grandmothers were obsessed with defying their age and had face lifts long before this practice was more common. My mom, at nearly 80, looks no older than 60. And my brother, after helping to invent a product that prevents people from looking older, is now quite literally working on the cure for aging.

(None of this is BS hyperbole. Google "Nathaniel David." Yep, one of the world's leading experts on anti-aging.)

I don't think it's an accident that my family is obsessed with not aging. We are a family, you see, that lives by another credo: the rules don't apply to us.

No one ever said this to me. They didn't need to because I absorbed it.

And what rule is more unfair and yet more unavoidable than aging?

My point is this: I always understood that aging would happen to *you*. I just thought I would stay eternally, say, 38, while you guys would get grey hair and clogged arteries and other, far worse things. Whenever I've spied a grey hair, I've felt inarguably, stupefyingly betrayed by my body. As I tweeze it and then pretend the whole thing never happened, I all but scream at the sky, "How could you do this to me?!"

And that brings me to my years of sobriety. While it's lovely in many ways to be sober for 18 years, that also means not being able to avoid one completely horrific fact: unless you got sober as a prepubescent, you simply can't be 18 years sober and not kinda, well, old.

But aging isn't the only horror I'd assumed I'd be able to avoid throughout my sobriety. I'd also had this idea that I'd be able to duck some of the other issues I'd heard other people discuss—namely, depression.

Now I understood from the beginning that it's not like you get sober and then things just get better and better all the time. I got that there were peaks and valleys only followed by more peaks and valleys. Still, at a certain point—SAY, 18 YEARS OF SOBRIETY—you sort of just maybe kind of think all that's *over*?

See, I'd heard early on that years seven through 10 of sobriety were not easy but I buckled through. Cool, I seemed to think, survived that, scratch it off the list, move on, share in meetings about the gifts of sobriety, keep meditating and praying and all that and the tides rise and stay there. Right?

Er, not really.

The bumps have continued and I feel as betrayed by them as I did by that grey hair I tweezed this morning. Don't all the happiness studies claim people get happier as they get older? Isn't that how I consoled myself over the fact that the aging rules *did* apply to me? When the fuck, I want to ask that deity that I seem to have a hard time finding when I'm going through the shit, does it just get *easy*?

Never have I been more gob-smacked by that question than early this summer, when early childhood trauma I'd spent a lifetime trying to avoid came screeching out. This all happened to come along at a time when I had truly established myself "out there" as a person who shared her dark to find her light. My company, Light Hustle Publishing, was successfully helping thought leaders write and publish and sell books. I had made my life philosophy clear in the world: if you share the things that have brought you the most shame, you will heal and help others to as well.

In a certain way, I was the perfect person to lead this charge. After all, I had been doing that since I published my first book about addiction in 2007.

For years, I'd been receiving accolades for my bravery when it came to sharing about my addiction. I've received hundreds of emails and social media messages and in person declarations from people who tell me that my podcast or something I've written or said has helped them to come to terms with their own addiction. They often add something like this: "Even though I may lose my family or career by coming clean, your bravery has given me the strength to do so."

For a long time, I accepted this praise, no questions asked. God damn it, was I a brave person, I would tell myself. And I didn't even have to try!

But that shield of self-congratulation I'd created to honor my bravery fell apart in the face of my summer breakdown. I am generally not a crier but I became someone who cried so hard, so publicly and so often that it wasn't even surprising one day when I was walking down the street, sobbing, and a homeless man asked me if I was all right. Humiliated, defensive, I responded, "Yes!" He looked at me, said, "You don't seem okay" and shuffled off.

It just happened that I had a book coming out at this time—a book I needed to go out there and promote. I dramatically told a friend one day between sob sessions that I couldn't be publicly together so I was going to cancel everything.

She shook her head. "I don't get you," she said. "This is your whole *thing*. Sharing your dark to find your light. Why wouldn't you be open about struggling?"

So I had to ask myself the same question. And that's when I saw that I'd never been ashamed about being an addict but I'd always been deeply, horribly ashamed about suffering from depression.

The truth, I suddenly saw, was that I seem to think sobriety is cool and that you, whoever you are, want to hear about it. I remember going to a restaurant early on in my sobriety, ordering a Diet Coke from a waiter and then adding, "The reason I'm ordering a soda and not a drink is that I'm newly sober after a crippling cocaine addiction and if I have a drink, that will just lead to more and next thing I know I'll be calling my dealer and then it will be 6 in the morning and I'll be wired to the gills, hearing the birds chirp and thinking about killing myself."

And I recall him nodding warily and, while backing away, telling me my soda was on the house.

Even if I haven't overshared about my addiction with you, I'm just a genre of person whom most people in the world would *expect* to be an addict. In LA, they say, you throw a rock and you'll either hit a sober person or someone who needs to get sober. People in recovery are so out and proud here that we don't even realize there's any other way to be. And writers? Well, we're *supposed* to be drowning out our senses to near incapacitation in order to access our creativity.

Point being: I was never going to *not* get a job because of having been addicted to drugs; if anything, it would help me *get* hired.

In other words, I wasn't nearly as brave as the people coming to me for help sharing their recovery stories.

I was a hypocrite.

Unlike a movie character's epiphany, however, I didn't have this realization and then change. This wasn't *Grease* and I wasn't

Sandy, ready to have Frenchie convert her from the person she'd been to the person she wanted to be.

In fact, when I signed on, puffy-eyed, to do a video interview the day after my friend confronted me, I told the person interviewing me that I had "just gotten some bad news" and might not be able to do the interview. This was about a month into my crying jag so the "bad news" was a lie.

Ignoring my attempt to duck out of the interview so I could surrender some more salt water from my eyes to the pillow, he said, "Well everyone here loves and supports you" and I realized that I wasn't just talking to a friend but to the *hundreds of people who had signed on early and were already watching online.* I felt humiliated.

The truth I had to face is that I only wanted to share dark experiences if they were in the past...that I wanted to look perfect but talk about a broken past so that I could be respected or even feel better than other people. "I struggled once, just like you're struggling now," I wanted to communicate. "But look at me now!" I wanted to have the ugliness be a funny or meaningful story from my past.

So I'm here from the front lines to report: I'm not cured. I still fall apart. And I can quote Leonard Cohen all I want and talk about how the crack is where the light comes in but the reality is it fucking sucks when I'm going through it. Even though, of course, just like all those people promised, I always come out on the other side having learned something invaluable. It just can take a long god damn time—unlike aging, which seems to happen in a millisecond.

In other words, it's taken me this long to truly accept the fact that the rules *do* apply to me. I even have the grey hairs to prove it.

Confessions of a So-So Sponsor

There are women I know who are excellent sponsors. They seem to have at least 10—usually more like 15—sponsees who call each other "sober sisters" and talk a lot about sponsorship lineage. These sponsors will share in meetings about how hearing from their sponsees is the highlight of their day because "it just takes me out of me." They call their sponsees their "babies," and smile lovingly as one after another of these babies thanks them through tears from the podium. They're the women that new girls are usually pushed toward when they first come into the rooms.

I am not one of these women.

At first, this bothered me. Until I faced one hard fact: I don't want 10-15 sponsees. Christ, I don't even know if I could handle five. I've got two right now and that feels like plenty.

Another fact: Most of the women I've sponsored have not stayed sober. This also used to bother me and I'd blame myself for not being better at this sponsorship thing. Then I remembered that most people don't stay sober, so maybe it was more a reflection of the challenges of maintaining sobriety than of a lack of skill on my part.

This isn't to say I don't enjoy sponsorship. I adored a sponsee I had for nearly five years when I lived in New York—but then I adored her before I ever sponsored her. Our road was hardly typical. It went like this: I heard her share in a meeting about how she'd dreamt that she'd been sold to a shepherd for marriage. I passed her a note that basically said, I don't know who you are but that dream is the funniest thing I've ever heard—can we be friends?

We went to dinner soon after, where she dropped what was, to a woman who thought she'd just found her BFF, a bombshell: She was just a few months sober. I had seven years myself, and suddenly felt like I was on a date with a guy who'd just revealed that he was 17. The newcomers I'd befriended since I'd put some time together had always turned out slightly, if not fully, insane. Amazing as this girl seemed, I told myself, she was not going to be my best friend. I felt almost heartbroken as we said goodnight. The next day, she called and, to my utter surprise, asked me to sponsor her.

Of course, it doesn't usually go like that. All the other sponsees I've had have approached me after hearing me share in a meeting; I've usually agreed to sponsor them before I've even gotten their name.

But when someone I really like comes to me with a sad story, a tale of someone who's treated her unfairly, I tend to immediately launch into what I always wanted my mom to do for me—telling her how right she is, how wrong that other person is, and how justified she is in her anger. I'm good at this: I know how to be a person's cheerleader when she doesn't quite see how to do that for herself. I know how to guide and advise; essentially, this is what makes me an awesome coach.

This, you may not need me to tell you, is not how sponsorship is supposed to work.

The truth is, I sometimes just don't know what to say to sponsees—especially when they're new. When I was new, I was emoting all over the place. But the newcomer women I tend to sponsor often tell me how great life is, how much they're enjoying sobriety and how everything's coming together beautifully—before pulling a disappearing act. I encourage them to share their ugliest realities, no matter how awkward it feels to do that with a near stranger, and they usually tell me they will. But the Pollyanna personality stays in place until the girl's eventual disappearing act. And there just isn't much I know to suggest to someone who's not telling me about any issues. I often have to remind myself that sometimes a sponsor's job is simply to listen.

That isn't to say I'm some Suzie Sunshine who lets sponsees get away with indulging their every whim. One girl I sponsored ignored everything I said to her about working the steps and would just call me when she was hysterical, mid-crisis (and she had a lot of crises).

One day, I calmly explained to her that I was not her on-call therapist, there to save her in the heat of every manic moment, but someone who was going to take her through the steps, so that she wouldn't feel like she needed someone to save her whenever she was in one of those moments. I never heard from her again. I can only hope I didn't scare her away from sobriety altogether.

Another girl I sponsored years ago started smoking pot again without telling me. When she finally came clean, I felt duped and frustrated. One evening soon after—back when I still had a landline—my phone rang all night long, every hour on the hour. Finally, at about 6 am, I picked up; it was the mother of this sponsee, calling me from Texas, hysterically explaining that her daughter was drunk and had asked her to call me. I said that I couldn't do anything for her daughter once she was drunk, and that I didn't think it made sense for me to be talking to my sponsee's mother whether my sponsee was drunk or sober. I asked her to not call me again. "I see why my daughter drank, with you as a sponsor!" she shrieked, before hanging up.

Like I said, I'm not in the running for any Best Sponsor awards. Not that that sponsee was in danger of winning any Best Sponsee awards, either.

Then there was the woman I sponsored who liked to argue with me on every point. My attitude about the argumentative ones is this: I'm not engaging in this process because I fancy a lively debate; I'm doing it because it saved my life and I hope it can save yours. I dreaded this girl's calls, but it seemed callous and harsh to tell her I couldn't sponsor her just because I didn't like her. One evening, she and I were in a meeting. I was knitting, as I sometimes do, and I needed to look up a knitting pattern on my phone. She was visibly irritated by the fact that I was doing something else while in a meeting. Afterwards, on the street, she unloaded on me. "How could you be on your phone during that meeting?!" she yelled. "You're supposed to be an example for me!"

I told her I wasn't perfect, that there were plenty of meetings where I didn't pay complete attention, and that I was there to take her through the steps, not to do everything exactly the way she thought I should. "You're fired!" she exclaimed as she stormed off.

I was simultaneously hurt and thrilled that I'd gotten off the hook. The next day, I got a message from her saying that she'd been thinking. Since she'd just finished her Fourth Step, maybe we could actually proceed with our plans and I could listen to it after all? Maybe, she added, we could work out this sponsorship thing?

I told her we couldn't, feeling very much like the universe had done for me what I hadn't been able to do for myself.

Was this the right thing to do? Who knows? Sponsorship may be one of the most variously interpreted aspects of the program. There's nothing in the Big Book about it and AA offers only one measly pamphlet on the topic, which doesn't say much. Are we supposed to keep sponsoring people if they relapse, or tell them to find someone new? Is it a good idea to have sponsees re-do the Steps every year, as some sponsors insist, or is once enough? What, exactly, should sponsees expect from us? One girl I agreed to sponsor called me soon after we met, while in the midst of a screaming fight with her husband. "Tell him how crazy he's being!" she demanded, before handing the phone over to him. I hung up. Maybe others would have played along; I sure didn't have any interest.

If it's unclear for sponsors, it's sure as hell unclear for the sponsees, too. All we're told when we get to program is to "look for someone who has what we want." Most of us are so befuddled when we arrive that we're not entirely clear on who we are, let alone what we want. My first sponsor—who ended up drinking when I had a year of sobriety, though she's back in the program now—stuck by me, and in many ways saved my life when I slipped at six-and-a-half months of sobriety. Others might have told me I hadn't surrendered and should find someone new.

We're all just doing the best we can with very little guidance. Still, to me, it's a miracle that the sponsorship process works at all.

What are the chances that you're going to find a person who's willing to take your calls, work with you on your problems, devote endless hours to you for no payment beyond the satisfaction that comes with helping someone the way they were helped, and the conviction that they must do it if they hope to stay sober? A zillion to one, maybe?

Right now, I have a sponsee who I love and adore—but the truth is we have more of a "let's go roller skating" or "let's go on a bike ride" relationship than one that involves me being of service. We just love to hang out and she doesn't require much, if any, official "sponsorship" from me. So are we the zillion to one partnership or am I shirking my duties by not pressing her to do more 10th steps or call me more? At this point, I have no idea.

When people share that they've been with the same sponsor for 10 or 20 or 30 years, I'm blown away. Yet it happens. And I've experienced my own miracles with sponsorship. I know I'm not ever going to be the woman who shares about how the best part of my day is hearing from one of my sponsees because "it just takes me out of me," but sponsoring has taught me boundaries and selflessness and a form of nurturing love that was entirely new to me.

And who knows, one day I may even get good at it.

SPECIAL BONUS! CHAPTER 1 EXCERPT FROM *PARTY GIRL*, SOON TO BE A MAJOR MOTION PICTURE

FROM *THE HOLLYWOOD REPORTER*, 11/1/2018:

MOVIES

'Silence' Exec Producer Acquires Anna David Novel 'Party Girl'

9:00 AM PDT 11/1/2018 by Mia Galuppo

Niels Juul picked up the book about a sober celebrity journalist who has to play the part of a party hopper.

Anna David's novel *Party Girl* has been acquired by Niels Juul, an exec producer on Martin Scorsese's *Silence* and *The Irishman*.

The novel centers around a celebrity journalist who, after years of hard partying, gets sober only to be hired by a glossy magazine to write a column about her party-hopping lifestyle.

The story closely parallels the life of David, who has been sober for nearly two decades. "I got a job writing a column called 'Party Girl' for [the now defunct] *Premiere* [magazine] right when I got out of rehab," she says. "And most of the misadventures in the book — especially the more ridiculous ones — are things I've experienced."

"When I read Anna's book I had one of those rare experiences of laughing out loud on one page and crying on the next, as I recognized so many good friends of mine from the fashion or movie business who either survived or surrendered to the late 90's party life and subsequent addictions," adds Juul. "It read like what *Sex and the City* would look like if it had a black sheep sister and had been written with hilarious ironic twists so relevant in today's reality-star-driven party world."

Party Girl

Copyright © 2007 by Anna David. All rights reserved. Printed in the United States of America. No part of this book may be used or reproduced in any manner whatsoever without written permission except in the case of brief quotations embodied in critical articles and reviews. For information, address HarperCollins Publishers, 10 East 53rd Street, New York, NY 10022.

CHAPTER 1

It is a truth universally acknowledged that crazy things happen at weddings. Or at least that's what I tell myself as my activities segue from outrageous to risqué to downright depraved.

There's the bathroom blow job incident, which I categorize as "outrageous" rather than "downright depraved," solely due to the fact that my eighty-two-year-old stepdad walks in while I'm going down on the cousin of the bride in the pool house bathroom. Because of his eighty-two-ness (the stepdad, not the cousin, thankfully), he was prone to more "senior moments" than non-senior moments—and thus is easily convinced that what had just happened never in fact happened. By the time I'm done talking to him, I've actually managed to convince him that not only was there no blow job, but also there had been no cousin of the bride. I'm pretty sure if I'd kept going I could have gotten him to believe there was no wedding. But the point is, in convincing my stepdad, I'm pretty sure I convince myself. And thus: outrageous, not downright depraved.

Don't bother asking me how I go from sitting next to the cousin and finding him mildly attractive—not gorgeous, just mildly attractive, someone I might have gone out with had he asked me—to kneeling down in front of him while he sat on Mom's bidet. It wouldn't have been my style to have asked, "Care for a blow job in the bath- room?" At least I don't think so. It's possible that after a bottle or so of good wedding champagne, Amelia Stone is replaced by Paris Hilton minus the millions, plus a good twenty pounds, but since my exploits haven't been caught on tape—note to exes, not that I know of—I can only venture this as a guess. I'd like to imagine that I happened to visit the restroom just as he was leaving and that our sudden passion erupted spontaneously. But by the end of the night—well, morning— the whole cousin incident was so comparatively pristine, I may as well have been a virgin in white in that bathroom.

Later, I find myself in the sauna with the groomsmen. It had been my mom's idea, that all the "young people" from the wedding should sauna and swim, but somehow it got down to just two guys and me. By this point, I know that I'm way more than mildly intoxicated, but since technically I'm on vacation, aren't I supposed to be? If I were this drunk in L.A., someone would probably bring out the coke and I'd thus be able to alleviate my alcohol buzz a bit, but parties at Mom's house tend to be pretty short on drugs—at least non-SSRI ones. And since in some ways there's no better high than having two men vying for your attention, I figure it's just as well that I'm not holding.

"I'm going to be graduating in May," Mitch says, as he offers me a sip of his warm Amstel Light. "Medical school has been a bitch."

"Oh, but now you're going to have to do your residency," Mitch's alleged best friend Chris interjects, while interjecting his body into the minuscule space that exists between Mitch and me. "You'll be working, like, ninety-hour weeks for no money."

"Which is so much worse than 'doing your residency' at Paramount for a salary just above the poverty line?" Mitch lobs back, looking at me.

I swear I never get tired of the attention of boys. But I prefer direct attention, rather than transparent male dick-swinging contests. Do they honestly think that the one who gets the last dig in will win my affection? Don't they know that being an assistant and a student, even a medical student, aren't exactly lady-killer positions to be in, and that they should perhaps be digging into their personal arsenals for more compelling things to compete over?

I stand up and they're silenced. "Last one in has to do a shot," I say and before I've even finished the sentence, they're pushing each other aside in their zeal to jump into the pool. I stand at the sauna door, cold air rushing in, their wet towels at my feet. If I didn't know better, I'd swear that the two of them just wanted to have sex with each other.

***

"Okay, we're going to sleep now," I instruct them, as I try to get as comfortable as I can while lodged between these two guys in a double bed. "Sleep."

I honestly think we're going to bed. Was anyone ever that naive? I can't even sleep on two Ambien by myself, but the birds are dangerously close to chirping—a horrifyingly depressing time to still be partying, as I've recently learned—this is the only bed left in the house, and neither of these guys are in any condition to drive. I turn toward Chris, who's facing the wall. Mitch is on the other side, facing the other wall.

A few minutes pass and I hear Mitch breathing heavily in that way that means he could be asleep. I sigh and feel more relaxed. My insomnia always seems embarrassing, and I'm all too relieved to be able to suffer through it without witnesses. Miraculously, I drift off for a moment or two.

And am awakened by lips on mine—specifically, lips belonging to Chris. My eyes swing open just in time for me to realize that Chris's kissing skills aren't half bad. Some people pride themselves on their gaydars. I pride myself on my kissdar because I can usually tell on sight if a guy is going to be one of those drench-your-face-with-saliva kissers, too-tentative pecking kissers, or a possessor of one of those lizard like tongues that darts into places it's not wanted. Most guys, unfortunately, fit into one of these categories. It's the ones that don't that drive us mad, in all the good ways.

Unfortunately, their kissing skills always seem to accompany a tendency for unemployment, a lack of an IQ, or just a general assholeishness. If they could kiss well and also possess qualities that actually made them good boyfriend material, women would probably maim and kill one another to have them. I had assumed that Chris would be some combination of too-tentative and lizard like—that he'd start out with inappropriate propriety and then swerve into too much without the required sensuality—and am startled to discover that he seems to know what he's doing. He even knows the take-my-face-in-his-hands move.

I kiss him back, enjoying the secretiveness of the act. Despite all their lame competitiveness, despite the fact that Chris is an assistant at Paramount and that he attacks his alleged best friend who's actually doing something useful with his life in a pathetic attempt to win a girl's affection, I'm more attracted to him than I am to Mitch.

Chris is kissing well enough that it's impossible to say how many times we kiss—one time just seems to mesh into another. And then I'm utterly shocked when I feel a hand creeping from behind into my nether region. Had Chris and Mitch, in some sort of a silent pact, targeted my two most manipulatable zones and decided to each work one of them? The thrill of kissing someone while another hand works me from behind is unbelievable. I'm completely getting off on the anonymity of the hand (even though I obviously know whose hand it is) and on this wise solution to all that petty male competitiveness that was going on earlier, until I come back to earth and remember where we are. Which is in the guest bedroom directly below my mom and stepdad's bedroom in their house, which I'm visiting for the week-end to see an old friend get married—not to blow his now-wife's cousin and have a ménage à trois with two of his groomsmen.

"Wait—you have to stop!" I suddenly screech. I jump out of bed and the two of them look alarmed, if not altogether shocked. I grab a pillow off the bed. "I need to go somewhere where I can actually sleep," I say, as if they'd been talking and I was tired of shushing them. Without another word, I stomp off to the den, where I promptly pass out on the couch.

DID YOU ENJOY THIS EXCERPT?

GET THE AUDIO VERSION OF *PARTY GIRL* ON **AUDIBLE** OR **AMAZON** FOR FREE WITH AN AUDIBLE TRIAL!

Get the book here: http://www.partygirlaudiobook.com/

Anna David is the *New York Times* and #1 Amazon bestselling author of two novels and five non-fiction books about addiction, recovery and relationships. She's been published in *The New York Times, Time, The LA Times, Vanity Fair, Playboy, Vice, Cosmo, People, Marie Claire, Redbook, Esquire, Self, Women's Health, The Huffington Post, Buzzfeed and Salon* among many others, written about in numerous publications, including *Forbes, Martha Stewart Living, Entrepreneur, Allure* and *Women's Health* and has appeared repeatedly on The *Today Show, Hannity, Attack of the Show, Dr. Drew, Red Eye, The Talk, The CBS Morning Show, The Insider* and numerous other programs on Fox News, NBC, CBS, MTV, VH1 and E.

She speaks at colleges across the country about relationships, addiction and recovery and has been a featured speaker at three different TedX events. Through her company, Light Hustle Publishing, she helps thought leaders write and publish books She also offers retreats, online courses, a podcast, a storytelling show and more.

Also by Anna David:

Party Girl

Bought

Reality Matters

Falling for Me

True Tales of Lust and Love

Are you wondering if you have a story to share?

Take this quiz: www.industryleaderquiz.com

Do you know you have a story to share but aren't sure if you should try to sell a proposal or self-publish?

Take this quiz: www.sellorselfpublish.com

Made in the USA
Middletown, DE
06 March 2019